TRANSPORT COMMITTEE

Fourth Report

RAILWAY FINANCES

Volume I

Report and Minutes of Proceedings

Ordered by The House of Commons *to be printed*
5 July 1995

LONDON: HMSO

£12.45 net

The Transport Committee is appointed under Standing Order No 130 to examine the expenditure, administration and policy of the Department of Transport and associated public bodies.

The Committee consists of 11 Members. It has a quorum of three. Unless the House otherwise orders, all Members nominated to the Committee continue to be members of it for the remainder of the Parliament.

The Committee has power:

(a)   to send for persons, papers and records, to sit notwithstanding any adjournment of the House, to adjourn from place to place, and to report from time to time;

(b)   to appoint specialist advisers either to supply information which is not readily available or to elucidate matters of complexity within the Committee's order of reference;

(c)   to communicate to any other committee appointed under the same Standing Order and to the Committee of Public Accounts and to the Deregulation Committee its evidence and any other documents relating to matters of common interest;

(d)   to meet concurrently with any other such committee for the purposes of deliberating, taking evidence, or considering draft reports.

The membership of the Committee since its nomination on 13 July 1992 has been as follows:

Mr Robert Adley (Chairman from 15 July 1992 to 13 May 1993), (deceased 13.5.93)

Mr Paul Channon (appointed 21 June 1993) elected Chairman 30 June 1993

Mr Jack Aspinwall
(discharged 15.12.92)
Mr Matthew Banks
Mr Peter Bottomley
Mr Terry Dicks
(discharged 7.12.92)
Mr Brian Donohoe
(appointed 25.1.93)
Mrs Gwyneth Dunwoody
Mr Nigel Evans
(appointed 15.12.92)
(discharged 5.7.93)
Mr Paul Flynn
(appointed 26.10.92)
Sir Alan Haselhurst

Mr Nick Hawkins
(appointed 7.12.92)
Mr James Hill
(appointed 6.12.93)
(discharged 24.1.95)
Mr Keith Hill
Mr Peter Luff
(appointed 5.7.93)
(discharged 6.12.93)
Mr John McFall
(discharged 26.10.92)
Mr Andrew Mackinlay
Sir David Madel
(appointed 24.1.95)
Mr David Marshall
(discharged 25.1.93)

The cost of printing and publishing this Report is estimated by HMSO at £3,828.
The cost of preparing for publication the Shorthand Minutes of Evidence published with this Report was £5,491.21.

TABLE OF CONTENTS

Page

List of Witnesses iv

List of Memoranda included in the Minutes of Evidence v

Table of Contents of the Report vi

Report vii

Proceedings of the Committee relating to the Report lvi

LIST OF WITNESSES

VOLUME II

Page

Wednesday 8 February 1995

BRITISH RAILWAYS BOARD

Sir Bob Reid, Mr J Jerram, Mr J Welsby, CBE and Mr A Nichols 79

Wednesday 15 February 1995

RAILTRACK PLC

Mr R Horton, Mr J Edmonds, Mr N Broadhurst, Mr D Moss and Mr D Rayner . . . 95

PASSENGER TRANSPORT EXECUTIVE GROUP

Mr S Lockley, Mr A Ritchie and Mr W Tyson 107

Wednesday 22 February 1995

OFFICE OF PASSENGER RAIL FRANCHISING

Mr R Salmon and Mr C Stokes 125

OFFICE OF THE RAIL REGULATOR

Mr J Swift, QC 133

CENTRAL RAIL USERS' CONSULTATIVE COMMITTEE

Major General Lennox Napier CB, OBE, Mr D Bertram, Sir Robert Wall
and Professor E Midwinter 139

Wednesday 1 March 1995

RAILWAY INDUSTRY ASSOCIATION

Mr D Gillan, Mr R Haines, Mr J Mills and Mr A Williams 145

GEC ALSTHOM

Dr K Lloyd 151

ABB

Mr E Drewery, Mr S Svärd and Mr R Harrison 154

Wednesday 8 March 1995

ASSOCIATION OF METROPOLITAN AUTHORITIES

Councillor M Dowd, Councillor M Lyons, Mr G Cook and Mr J Jenkins 159

Wednesday 15 March 1995

DEPARTMENT OF TRANSPORT

The Rt Hon Dr Brian Mawhinney, MP 175

Thursday 8 June 1995

DEPARTMENT OF TRANSPORT

The Rt Hon Dr Brian Mawhinney, MP 237

LIST OF MEMORANDA
INCLUDED IN THE MINUTES OF EVIDENCE

VOLUME II

Pages

Press Notice from the Transport Committee 1
1. Department of Transport 1
2. British Railways Board 10
3. Office of Passenger Rail Franchising (OPRAF) 16
4. Railtrack PLC 18
5. Office of the Rail Regulator 22
6. Central Rail Users' Consultative Committee 27
7. Passenger Transport Executive Group 44
8. Railway Industry Association 57
9. York City Council .... 69&72
10. York Area Economic Development Unit 71
11. The Institution of Railway Signal Engineers 75
12. Mr R Harman and Professor B Atkin 76
13. Further Memorandum from OPRAF 117
14. Letter from the Transport Committee to the Department of Transport 169
15. Letter from the Department of Transport 173
16. Further Memorandum from the Department of Transport 173
17. Letter from Railtrack PLC 174
18. Letter from the British Railways Board 174
19. Further Memorandum from Railtrack PLC 188
20. Further Memorandum from the York Area Economic Development Unit ... 190
21. Letter from the Central Rail Users' Consultative Committee 194
22. Transport 2000 (London & South East Region) 194
23. Further Memorandum from the British Railways Board (summary of the
    Hesketh Report) 201
24. Further letter from Railtrack PLC 205
25. Further Memorandum from OPRAF 205
26. Further Memorandum from Railtrack PLC 208
27. Further letter from Railtrack PLC 209
28. Further Memorandum from the British Railways Board 212
29. Letter from Mr Hugh Bayley MP 218
30. Correspondence between Merseytravel and the Department of Transport ... 218
31. Memorandum from The Institution of Civil Engineers 222
32. Further Memorandum from the Department of Transport 224
33. Letter from the West Midlands Passenger Transport Authority 225
34. Memorandum from the Association of Metropolitan Authorities 226
35. Memorandum from ABB 228
36. Letter from Mr H Raven 230
37. Letter from Mr J Farquharson OBE 230
38. Press Notice from OPRAF 232
39. Letter from the Transport Committee to and reply from the Department
    of Transport 234
40. Letter from the Department of Transport to the AMA 234
41. Letter from the Greater Manchester Passenger Transport Authority to the
    Department of Transport 235
42. Further letter from the British Railways Board 236

TABLE OF CONTENTS OF THE REPORT

Page

I   INTRODUCTION vii

II   THE STATE OF RAILWAY FINANCES viii
      British Rail's Finances up to 31 March 1994 viii
      British Rail's Finances in 1994-95 xii
      Railtrack's Finances in 1994-95 and beyond xv
      Privatisation Effects xvi
      Support for passenger services in 1997-98 xvii
      Assurance of subsidy to franchisees xx

III   LOCALLY SUPPORTED SERVICES xxi

IV   FREIGHT xxvi

V   INVESTMENT AND MAINTENANCE xxviii
      Total Railway Investment xxviii
      Railtrack's Maintenance and Investment Programme xxx
      Maintenance and Investment Levels and Equipment Orders xxxi
          Signalling Equipment xxxi
          Trackwork xxxiii
      Rolling Stock xxxv
      Major Projects xxxvii
      The Private Finance Initiative xxxvii

VI   THE PROSPECTS FOR EFFICIENCY AND REVENUE IMPROVEMENTxxxviii
      Changes arising from Restructuring xxxviii
      The Prospect of Efficiency Gains xxxix
      Prospects for Revenue Generation xl

VII   PRIVATISATION COSTS xlii

VIII CONCLUSIONS xlv
      Railway Finances from 1994-95 to 1996-97 xlv
      Railway Finances in 1997-98 xlvi
      Passenger Service Requirements xlvii
      Government Support for Railway Services xlviii
      Administrative Costs of Privatisation xlviii
      The Role of the Regulator xlix
      Locally Supported Services xlix
      Freight l
      Investment li
          Infrastructure li
          Rolling Stock lii
      Major Projects lii
      Summary of Conclusions and Recommendations liii
      Glossary of Abbreviations lv

FOURTH REPORT

RAILWAY FINANCES

The Transport Committee has agreed to the following Report:

I INTRODUCTION

1. It is two years since the Transport Committee published its substantial report on railway privatisation.[1]   Since then we have held evidence sessions reviewing the progress of privatisation with Railtrack plc and with the Rail Regulator and the Franchising Director.[2] We also received evidence on railways from the former Secretary of State during sessions on the Department of Transport's Annual Reports of 1993 and 1994.[3]

2. In the White Paper which launched railway privatisation the Government's objective was said to be "to extend the involvement of the private sector in the operation of the railways, ensure continuity of services, assure safety, and provide value for money. This is the best way to improve the service to customers".[4] As we noted in our 1993 Report, the explanatory notes to the Railways Bill indicated that privatisation was "not expected to lead to major reductions in public expenditure in the short term". While the Government undertook to continue to provide grant to support socially necessary services, it nevertheless anticipated that "private sector operation should, over time, allow railway services to be provided at a lower cost to the Exchequer than would otherwise have been the case". It was not an objective of the Government that Treasury support for the railways should decrease.[5] The Transport Committee's conclusion, having examined the proposals, was that "there must be a possibility that …. the cost to the taxpayer of providing the same level of services will actually rise. This is irrespective of the case we have argued for higher investment in the railway system."[6]

3. Towards the end of 1994 we were concerned that the effects on revenues of the recession, the signal workers' strike in summer 1994, the loss of coal traffic, the late opening of the Channel Tunnel and certain costs associated with privatisation and restructuring might mean that the railway operators would be short of the money they needed to operate services at the current level. We also wished to consider the level of current and planned investment in the railway, particularly in the infrastructure.

4. We therefore decided on 7 December 1994 to inquire into the state of railway finances in order to:

— identify whether any threat existed to existing passenger or freight services as a result of lack of funds;

— judge the adequacy of current and planned levels of maintenance and of renewals of infrastructure and rolling stock, and the state of the railway supply industry; and

— determine the effect upon public finances of privatisation.

During our inquiry we heard oral evidence from British Rail, Railtrack, representatives of Passenger Transport Executives and Passenger Transport Authorities, the Franchising Director, the Rail Regulator, the Central Rail Users' Consultative Committee, members of

---

[1]*The Future of the Railways in the Light of the Government's White Paper Proposals*, HC (1992-93) 246.

[2]HC (1992-93) 879-i and HC (1993-94) 120-i.

[3]HC (1992-93) 772 and HC (1993-94) 323-i.

[4]*New Opportunities for the Railways,* DoT 1992, (Cm 2012).

[5]HC (1992-93) 246, paragraphs 25 and 49.

[6]*Ibid*, paragraph 501.

the railway supply industry and, on two occasions, the Secretary of State for Transport. We received written evidence from these sources and from several others. We are very grateful to all our witnesses for the help they have given us in providing information about this complex and changing subject. The data used in compiling this report was the best available to us at 30 June 1995.

5. During this inquiry we have been aided by our two specialist advisers on railway matters, Professor Bill Bradshaw of the Centre for Socio-Legal Studies, Wolfson College, Oxford, and Mr Richard Hope, railway journalist and consultant. We are most grateful to them for their assistance.

6. This report describes the state of railway finances in recent years, at the moment and as they are expected to be in future years. It then considers the question of continuing local authority support for passenger services, the privatisation of freight businesses, investment and maintenance levels and, finally, the costs of privatisation and the possibilities of efficiency and revenue improvements as a result. The Committee's conclusions and recommendations on these matters are presented in Section VIII (paragraph 134 onwards).

II THE STATE OF RAILWAY FINANCES

7. Our primary concern has been to determine whether railway finances are likely to be adequate to maintain the present level of services in the short to medium term, and to prevent deterioration of the physical condition of the national rail network in the longer term. To form a basis for this judgement, we examined in particular three periods:

— the years leading up to March 31 1994 when BR operated in its traditional manner as a vertically integrated railway;

— the year ending 31 March 1995 (1994-95) when Railtrack was a separate government-owned company throughout and European Passenger Services followed suit on 8 May 1994; essential elements of the railway remained in the public sector but grant support for passenger services was increased to fund 'profits' which both BR and Railtrack returned to Government (see Figure 1, p.xiii);

— the year ending 31 March 1998 (1997-98) by which time it is planned that privatisation will be complete under the Government's programme, except perhaps for a minority of passenger services not yet franchised (See Figure 2, p.xix).

We have not looked in detail at 1995-96 or 1996-97. This is because the Government's expenditure plans announced in November 1994 include as "privatisation effects" contributions from the sale of parts of the rail business which are undisclosed and, of necessity, somewhat arbitrary.[7] Hence it would be difficult to form a view on the adequacy during those years of the External Finance Limit for the national railways.

British Rail's Finances up to 31 March 1994

8. The last major change in the way British Rail (BR) was financed occurred in 1974.[8] Between 1974 and 1994, Passenger Service Obligation (PSO) grant was paid to BR by the Department of Transport (DoT) to bridge the gap between total passenger revenues and the cost of maintaining services broadly at the level prevailing in 1974. The cost of maintaining lines used by passengers (more than 90% of the network) was essentially covered by the PSO grant. Freight was expected to pay its way operationally, and to cover the cost of freight-only lines, but was charged for the use of passenger lines on a marginal cost basis.

9. InterCity routes ceased to benefit from PSO grant from 1 April 1988, when BR was enjoying a period of comparative prosperity. Despite the onset of recession, the InterCity

---

[7]Evidence, p.3, para 23.
[8]Railways Act 1974.

business remained profitable throughout the six years to 1993-94, managing to turn in an operating profit of £98m in its final year as a business entity. From 1988-89, only Network SouthEast and Regional Railways received PSO grant, a proportion of which was intended to cover investment in asset renewal. Regional Railways also received grant from the seven Passenger Transport Executives, and small sums from other local authorities. Trainload Freight was generally profitable but Railfreight Distribution and parcels were not.[9]

10. In addition to PSO and other grants, BR was able to borrow from the National Loans Fund (NLF) to cover investment and losses on its unsubsidised businesses. The combined total of grant and loans in any year is subject to the External Finance Limit (EFL) which is set each November by the Chancellor of the Exchequer in his Budget Statement. The actual total on a historic basis is known as the External Finance Requirement (EFR). In recent years, the EFR has been much higher than the PSO grant, notably in 1992-93 when the EFR peaked at £2,170m and the PSO grant also peaked at £1,214m, both at 1994-95 prices.[10] Annexes A and B1 of the DoT's evidence, reproduced below, show recent and planned Government support to the railways:

TABLE 1[11]

Government support to the Railways
External Finance[1]
1985-86—1997-98

	BR/RT EFR		UR/EPS EFR		Grant[2]	Industry EFR	
	£ million cash	£ million 94-5 prices	£ million cash	£ million 94-5 prices	£ million cash	£ million cash	£ million 94-5 prices
85-86	910	1,414				910	1,414
86-87	777	1,172				777	1,172
87-88[3]	545	781				545	781
88-89	376	505				376	505
89-90	646	811	65	82		711	892
90-91	917	1,065	160	186		1,077	1,251
91-92	1,135	1,241	329	360		1,464	1,600
92-93	1,606	1,688	458	481		2,064	2,170
93-94	1,033	1,054	428	437		1,461	1,490
94-95[4]	-645	-645	217	217	1,924	1,496	1,496
95-96[5]	-945		120		1,800	975	
96-97[5]	to be decided				to be decided	810	
97-98[5]	to be decided				to be decided	810	

Notes:
1. The Government gives BR compensation to support socially necessary services which are not self-financing, and allows BR to borrow money at favourable rates of interest from the National Loans Fund, and from other sources, (eg. the European Investment Bank) if these provide value for money. This combination of grant and borrowing is known as the External Financing Limit (EFL), and is a measure of Government support for the railways.
2. Estimated grant support to passenger services from 1994-95 includes Franchising Director Grant and Metropolitan Railway Grant for PTE services.
3. Outturns (External Finance Requirements: EFRs) from 1987-88 have been restated to reflect a technical decision taken in PES 92 to exclude movements in payroll creditors from BR's EFL. In some years the restated outturn is greater than that reported in BR's Annual Report and Accounts. This does not represent an overspend in those years.
4. External Finance Limit. This figure was increased in-year by £259 million to £1,496 million and may increase by a further £64 million to £1,560 million.
5. Privatisation effects not shown. Future EFLs are in cash prices and include an estimated £70 million of grant paid by Scottish Office via PTEs to BR.

[9]BR annual reports.
[10]Evidence, p.4-5.
[11]Evidence, p.4, Annex A.

TABLE 2[12]

Government support to the Railways
Public Service Obligation Grant[1]
1985-86—1994-95

	£ million cash	£ million 94-95 prices
1985-86	820	1,274
1986-87	714	1,077
1987-88	794	1,137
1988-89	473	635
1989-90	501	629
1990-91	602	699
1991-92	892	975
1992-93	1,155	1,214
1993-94	930	949
1994-95[2]	1,700	1,700

Notes:
1. Until 1 April 1994 BR received Public Service Obligation Grant to support certain passenger services. PSO grant is allowed under EC rules and subsidised loss making but socially desirable services on Regional Railways and Network South East (and InterCity up to 1987-88). It covered both capital spending (investment) and current spending (running costs).
2. From 1994-95, grant support to passenger services paid by the Franchising Director. The figure for 1994-95 is an estimate. Figures are not available for future years.

11. A basic principle of the financing arrangements introduced from 1 April 1994 is that the national railways no longer draw loans from the Government as well as receiving grants. Instead, a larger subsidy is paid to franchised passenger operators, who are thus enabled to contract with private companies for track, rolling stock and other facilities. These companies are able to attract private capital for investment because "since 1 April 1994, trading between the various components of the restructured railway has allowed them to earn proper commercial returns like any other business".[13] With privatisation complete, the only circumstances in which Government funds might be made available directly for investment would be for "schemes which cannot earn an adequate financial return, but provide a satisfactory cost-benefit return when wider benefits are taken into account".[14] These would be grants, however, not loans.

12. Since nationalisation in 1948, loans to the railways have had to be suspended or written off in 1962, 1968 and 1974. Clearly, borrowing from the NLF involves a risk that the railways will not be able to repay the loan. However, private risk capital generally requires higher rates of interest than NLF loans. By transferring responsibility for investment to Railtrack, the Rolling Stock Companies (ROSCOs) and other private companies such as maintenance depot operators, the Government avoids financial risk in return for a premium in the form of higher subsidy.

13. In attempting to assess the potential value to the Government of this risk transfer, we noted that from 1990-91 to 1993-94 net borrowing by BR ranged from £368m to £894m a year; at the same time, PSO grant also rose substantially, peaking at £1,214m in 1992-93 before dropping back to £949m in the final year of the old regime (all at 1994-95 prices).[15] At first sight, this presents a classic picture of railway finances out of control, as in the 1960s.

14. However, further examination reveals that in 1988-89 the EFL was only £505m at 1994-95 prices, lower than the grant total at £629m which meant that BR was actually

---

[12]Evidence, p.5, Annex B1

[13]Evidence, p.2, para 11.

[14]HC (1992-93) 246-IV, p.299.

[15]Evidence, p.5, Annex B1.

reducing its debt.[16] BR's outstanding loans only amounted to £112m on 1 April 1991, although they had risen to £2,484m by 1 April 1994. In fact, BR did not borrow at all for 10 years up to 1990-91.[17] So BR was living within its means in the 1980s and was not, in fact, being subsidised through loans that might or might not be repaid.

15. This position would not have been tenable if BR had failed to invest in renewals of infrastructure and rolling stock. In fact, when Channel Tunnel related investment is excluded, the amount spent in the six years from 1987-88 to 1992-93 was almost exactly equal to the steady state requirement defined by BR Chairman Sir Bob Reid as "around £1bn per annum" at current prices.[18] However, it presumably was not sufficient to correct significant under-investment in the period from 1966 to 1986.[19]

16. There are two principal reasons why the EFR quadrupled in real terms between 1988-89 and 1992-93: works connected with the Channel Tunnel and the recession. Moreover, although the EFR dropped back sharply from £2,170m to £1,490m (at 1994-95 prices) in 1993-94, this was achieved largely by a cutback in investment in the domestic railway (that is, excluding Channel Tunnel services) from a reasonably stable £1bn over the previous three years to only £665m.[20]

17. With the onset of recession, real income from InterCity and Network SouthEast ticket sales fell by 13% and 4% respectively between 1990-91 and 1993-94, and the annual November count in 1994 showed commuting into London 19% below the 1989 peak.[21] The collapse of the 1980s property boom also had a major impact on BR's finances. In 1989-90 the net contribution from property was £412m but by 1992-93 it was only £158m, reducing internal funds available to invest in the railway by well over £200m in real terms.[22] And finally, freight revenue was affected not only by the recession but also by the switch from coal to other fuels for electricity generation, falling from £594m to £442m (at 1994-95 prices) between 1990-91 and 1993-94.[23]

18. Expenditure on preparations for the Channel Tunnel has placed a severe strain on BR finances since 1989-90. From then until 1993-94, the outflow of funds in respect of what became European Passenger Services (which runs Eurostar) and Union Railways (which is promoting the high speed link to London) totalled £1,546m at 1994-95 prices.[24] Adding in the amount spent in respect of Channel Tunnel freight lifts this figure to some £2 billion. As at 1 April 1994, there had been no compensating revenue because the Channel Tunnel was not open.

19. No grant was payable towards this investment because this was specifically prohibited under section 42 of the Channel Tunnel Act 1987. Had it not been for the Channel Tunnel, BR's capital debt might have been under £500m on 1 April 1994, a not unreasonable amount for a business turning over £3.6 billion which had demonstrated in the 1980s an ability to reduce its debt when the economy was buoyant, and had reduced its basic costs by 6.5% in real terms during the previous three years.[25]

20. To sum up, it would appear that BR had managed to achieve and hold a position of financial stability, so far as the domestic railway was concerned, through the 'boom' years of the late 1980s and the recession which followed, although investment and spending had to

---

[16]Evidence, p.4, Annex A and B1.

[17]Evidence, p.7, Annex C.

[18]Q2. Investment figures are given in Table 4 below (p.xxix).

[19]HC (1992-93) 246, Figure 2 p xl.

[20]Evidence, p.12, Table 8.

[21]Evidence, p.11, para 7.

[22]BR annual reports.

[23]Evidence, p.11, Table 4.

[24]Evidence, p.4, Annex A.

[25]Evidence, p.12, Table 6.

be cut drastically in the final year of the old regime in order to stay within the EFL.[26] During this period we found no evidence of 'hidden subsidy' to the domestic railway either from significant under-investment or excessive borrowing to supplement the PSO grant.

British Rail's Finances in 1994-95

21. On 1 April 1994 the whole financial picture was transformed. Railtrack became a government owned company and charged BR's train operating units (TOUs), passenger and freight, for the use of the track. Passenger carriages and locomotives were transferred to three new Rolling Stock Companies (ROSCOs), still within BR ownership, which leased them back to the TOUs at a total cost of £800m a year. BR ceased initiating significant amounts of investment beyond honouring existing contracts, mainly for rolling stock,[27] because Railtrack had assumed responsibility for all infrastructure spending and European Passenger Services was responsible for investment in international trains. The management and workforce responsible for maintaining the infrastructure was formed into BR Infrastructure Services (BRIS) units which are paid as contractors by Railtrack.

22. Railtrack and the various units still within BR now operate as though they were commercial companies. That is, they are responsible for funding their own investment (if any) from the payments they receive, and must produce a profit which is paid back to Government as the sole shareholder. The effect is to create a circular flow of money from the Government through the Office of Passenger Rail Franchising (OPRAF) and the Passenger Transport Executives (PTEs) to the TOUs, and then to Railtrack and the ROSCOs, with a proportion representing the profit (or 'dividends' which future investors in these companies might expect) passing back to Government. The principal flows of money which actually circulated within this 'circular cash flow' in 1994-95 are shown in Figure 1 below.

---

[26]Evidence, p.10, Table 1.
[27]QQ107-108.

FIGURE 1

The circular cash flow in 1994–95
(at 1994–95 prices)

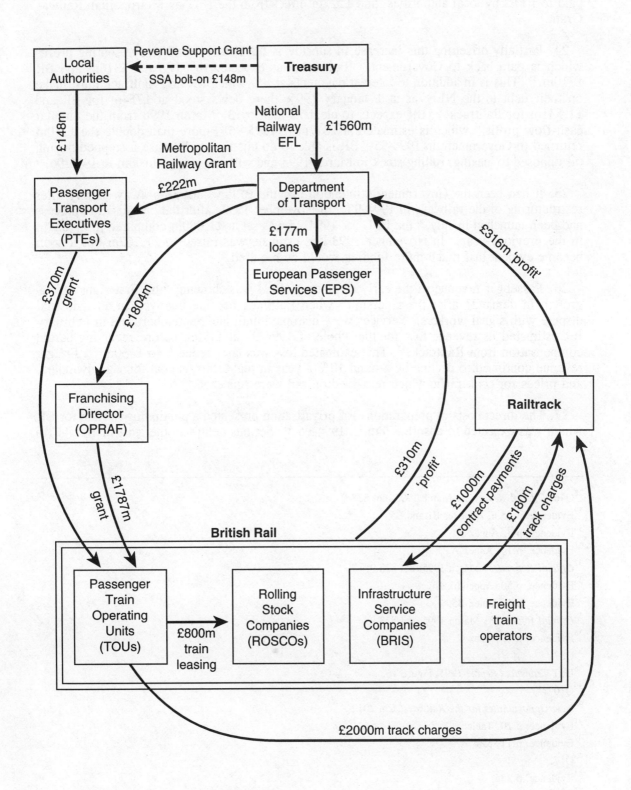

23. The increase in subsidy necessary to establish this structure has proved to be substantial, and estimates of the amount required rose during the year. The total of grants from OPRAF and the PTEs appears to be £2,157m, as shown in Figure 1.[28] This compares with £1,073m in PSO and PTE grants received by BR in 1993-94.[29] The grant due to be paid by OPRAF to the TOUs in 1994-95 was estimated in early 1995 at £1,700m by the DoT[30] and £1,725m by BR.[31] A more recent announcement implies that the OPRAF subsidy was in the end £1,787m (£2,009m minus the Metropolitan Railway Grant of £222m.)[32] To this must be added grant paid by the PTEs which they put at £356m[33] and DoT put at £372m (subsequently revised downwards by £2m).[34] This is made up of £148m paid to PTEs by local authorities, and £222m direct from the DoT as Metropolitan Railway Grant.

24. Partially offsetting this increase in subsidy is the flow of funds, representing profit, which is paid back to Government. Railtrack was expected to pay back £316m and BR £310m.[35] This is in addition to interest payments at 8% which BR and Railtrack must make on their debt to the NLF; as at 1 January 1995, these debts stood at £754m for BR and £1,531m for Railtrack.[36] BR expects to clear its debt by 31 March 1996 from the circular cash flow profit,[37] which is estimated at £817m in 1995-96[38], more than double the £310m returned to Government in 1994-95. BR is able to do this mainly because it stopped buying (as opposed to leasing) rolling stock in March 1995 and will only invest £100m in 1995-96.[39]

25. It had been the Government's intention that the EFR would drop away sharply after restructuring of the railways in 1994-95. In November 1992, after the privatisation process had been launched in July,[40] the EFL for 1994-95 was set at £1,080m compared to £1,529m in the previous year. In November 1993 this estimate was raised to £1,262m but it soon became evident that much more funding would be required.[41]

26. Passenger revenue in the early summer of 1994 was showing "the first signs of real growth in demand" after the recession[42] when Railtrack became involved in an industrial dispute with signal workers. Services were disrupted until late September, and in February BR estimated its revenue loss for the whole of 1994-95 at £170m before receiving partial compensation from Railtrack.[43] This estimated loss was later reduced to £150m.[44] Freight revenue continued to decline by around 10% a year in real terms as coal tonnage dwindled, and prices for coal traffic which remained on rail were squeezed.[45]

27. The direct costs of preparations for privatisation presented a continuing burden for BR which was expected to absorb £78m in 1994-95.[46] Serious delays in the start of freight (to

---

[28] Q46; *Official Report*, 31 March 1995, col 828-9.

[29] Evidence, pp.5-6, Annexes B1 and B5.

[30] Evidence, p.5, Annex B1.

[31] Evidence, p.14, Annex A.

[32] *Official Report*, 31 March 1995, col 828-9.

[33] Evidence, p.50, Appendix 4.

[34] Evidence, p.6, Annex B5.

[35] *Official Report*, 31 March 1995, col 828-9.

[36] Evidence, p.7, Annex C.

[37] Q87.

[38] DoT *Transport Report 1995*, Figure 16.

[39] Q107.

[40] *New Opportunities for the Railways*, Cm 2012.

[41] Evidence, p.10, Table 1.

[42] Evidence, p.11, para 7.

[43] Q17.

[44] Evidence, p.236.

[45] Evidence, p.11, paras 8-10.

[46] Evidence, p.11, para 11.

1 June) and passenger (to 14 November) services through the Channel Tunnel also cost BR an estimated £80m in lost revenue during 1994-95.[47]

28. By October 1994, it was obvious that the EFL of £1,262m set the previous November would be insufficient, and that the requirement was in fact closer to £1,700m; no revision of the EFL had been agreed by Government, however. It was this situation which led the Committee to undertake this inquiry. Faced with a potential shortfall of some £400m in 1994-95, and a similar deficiency in the following year, managers within BR were asked to consider what they would need to do and what it would mean for services if they were faced with a 10% cut in available finance. The then BR Chairman, Sir Bob Reid, told us that in December (eight months into the financial year) "the budget was then discussed with the Secretary of State yet again to try and reach a final conclusion, not only as to what the EFL for the industry would be, but how that would be divided across the main components of the industry which are Railtrack, ourselves and EPS".[48]

29. The outcome was an increase in the EFL to £1,496m. BR agreed to find expenditure reductions of £160m, and Railtrack £40m, in order to close the remaining gap of £200m. Late in January, the EFL was effectively relaxed by a further £64m to £1,560m through a concession that allowed BR to reduce the sum it then had to repay in circular cash flow profit from £301m to £237m,[49] although the Government continued to regard £1,496m as the formal EFL.[50]

30. As regards 1995-96, although we have not attempted a full analysis of finances in that year, we were somewhat reassured to learn that the BR Board "now believes that it will be possible to deliver services broadly comparable with the current timetable".[51]

Railtrack's Finances in 1994-95 and beyond

31. Railtrack's income in 1994-95 is expected to be £2.4 billion, 80% of which (£2 billion) comes from the passenger TOUs in track access charges. Most of the remainder comes from freight access charges (£180m) and property (£160m).[52] A decision announced by the Regulator on 17 January 1995 requires Railtrack to reduce its access charges for franchised passenger services (which covers all of BR's scheduled services) by 8% in 1995-96 on average in real terms compared with charges levied in 1994-95. They must then be reduced by 2% in each of the five subsequent years.[53]

32. Railtrack's costs in 1994-95 were stated to be £800m on maintenance of the infrastructure, mainly by BRIS; £570m on renewals; £400m on its own operations which include signalling and train control; and £300m on electricity for traction, cumulo rates, and the British Transport Police.[54] This leaves "an operating profit before interest, tax and exceptional items of £300m".[55] As the interest being paid on the £1,531m of NLF loans and other debt amounts to "approximately £150m",[56] we asked the Department how Railtrack was able to pay to Government in 1994-95 the £316m in circular cash flow profit required to meet the EFL target.[57] We were told that

---

[47]Evidence, p.13, para 18.

[48]Q26.

[49]Q30.

[50]DoT Transport Report 1995, footnote 3 to Fig 16.

[51]Evidence, p.13, para 23.

[52]Evidence, p.19-20, para 13.

[53]Railtrack's Access Charges for Franchised Passenger Services, Office of the Rail Regulator, January 1995.

[54]Evidence, p.20, para 16. [Cumulo rates are a proxy for business rates.]

[55]Q124.

[56]Q124.

[57]Official Report, 31 March 1995, col 828-9.

"there is a difference between Railtrack's profit and the assessment of its EFC [External Finance Contribution]. Factors such as movements in working capital will affect the company's EFC, but will be neutral in terms of its profit and loss account. Therefore, there is no inherent contradiction in the fact that — for a given year — Railtrack could have a profit level different from its EFC. The Committee will no doubt have noted that the Railtrack chairman's opening remarks were intended to give a general picture of the business and were not meant to show performance in a particular year. Railtrack will publish audited accounts for 1994/95 later this year."[58]

33. Railtrack's Chairman, Mr Robert Horton, made it clear to us that he was not at this stage able to give very precise figures for future years because his Business Plan was in the process of revision following the Regulator's decision a few days earlier on access charges for franchised passenger operators. The plan submitted to the Regulator to inform his decision contained "commercially confidential information which will be sensitive in the run-up to quotation on the Stock Exchange".[59]

34. As regards 1995-96, Mr Horton stressed that "getting 8% off our real costs in the first year, which is the flip side of getting 8% off access charges, is going to be quite a challenge".[60] In fact, the Government is expecting Railtrack's circular cash flow profit to drop from £316m in 1994-95 to £128m in 1995-96, a reduction of £188m.[61] As the 8% reduction in access charges ordered for 1995-96 amounts to £160m, the challenge to cut costs is perhaps not as severe as it seems. Likewise, subsidy payments to Train Operating Companies, through OPRAF and the PTEs, drop by £209m from £2,009m in 1994-95 to £1,800m in 1995-96.[62] In other words, the 8% access charge reduction has simply been knocked off the profit target previously set for Railtrack included in the circular cash flow. This has no practical effect, but will reduce the value of Railtrack to potential investors.

Privatisation Effects

35. As already explained (para 7), the Government's expenditure plans announced last November for the three years 1995-96 to 1997-98 are difficult to interpret because of a new entry described as "National Railways Privatisation Effects". These amount to -£770m and -£325m in 1995-96 and 1996-97, the minus sign implying a flow of money from the railways to Government. In 1997-98, however, the amount shown is £600m, the absence of a minus sign indicating that the money flows from Government into the railways.[63]

36. Privatisation Effects are described by the DoT as "the net sum of a nominal estimate of proceeds from the sale of the ROSCOs and other businesses (excluding Railtrack), and the loss of the external finance contributions of ROSCOs, Railtrack and other businesses as a consequence of their privatisation".[64] In addition, "the estimates underlying these figures are commercially confidential".[65]

37. As already noted (para 24), BR's payment back to Government is expected to rise from £310m in 1994-95 to £817m in 1995-96.[66] In 1995-96 much of this will be used to extinguish its debt to the NLF (which stood at £754m on 1 January 1995), and so will not be profits paid to the Department of Transport. The sales of BR subsidiaries likely to generate most cash (the ROSCOs and BRIS) are not expected to take place until well into the second

---

[58]Evidence, p.234.

[59]Evidence, p.18.

[60]Q136.

[61]*Official Report*, 31 March 1995, col 828-9, DoT *Transport Report 1995* Fig16.

[62]*Official Report*, 31 March 1995, col 828-9, DoT *Transport Report 1995,* Fig 16.

[63]DoT *Transport Report 1995*, Figure 2.

[64]We understand this to mean that if, by way of illustration, the three ROSCOs were sold during 1995-96 for £2,000m, and as a consequence the amount of circular cash flow profit that the Government would have received from BR during that year was reduced by £200m, then the Privatisation Effects of these transactions would be -£1,800m in that year and £200m in each following year since the loss of profit would be permanent.

[65]Evidence, p.3, para 23.

[66]DoT *Transport Report 1995* Figure 16; *Official Report*, 31 March 1995, col 828-9.

half of 1995-96. Until these sales are completed, the companies will continue to remit profits to BR which passes them on to Government. It appears unlikely, therefore, that the loss of profit to BR resulting from sales occurring late in 1995-96 could amount to much more than £100m, as in addition the companies concerned do not account for all of BR's surplus, some of which is generated by the Train Operating Units (we have assumed that the first TOUs will not begin operation in the private sector until the beginning of financial year 1996-97).

38. As the Privatisation Effects for 1995-96 have been estimated by the Government at -£770m, and the offsetting loss of revenue to BR is relatively small, it follows that the anticipated sales proceeds must be less than £1 billion. As the gross revenues of the ROSCOs, BRIS, BRIML and Trainload Freight exceed £2 billion a year, with the first two virtually guaranteed an appropriate level of profit, and they are to be sold by 31 March 1996,[67] the question arises as to why the expected proceeds of sales planned for 1995-96 are apparently so low.

39. One reason could be that some of the proceeds of sales planned for 1995-96 are deferred into 1996-97. But Privatisation Effects for 1996-97 are only -£325m, so combined Privatisation Effects for the two years are -£1.1 billion. There is no estimate for payments by BR back to Government in 1996-97, but obviously the profits accruing to BR will be greatly reduced if sales proceed as planned. What is not clear is the benchmark against which the Government assesses the 'loss of profit' element of Privatisation Effects, ie whether it is the £817m to be paid in 1995-96, or the £310m paid in 1994-95. Without this information, it is not possible to form a judgement on the anticipated proceeds of the sales, nor the funds available to BR in these two financial years to operate services for which it is still responsible.

Support for passenger services in 1997-98

40. We decided to set aside this conundrum and accept at face value assurances from the Secretary of State that BR, Railtrack and the Franchising Director "would have enough resources to run the railways next year".[68] However, according to the Government's plans, franchising of more than half the passenger services (by revenue) is to be complete by 1 April 1996, most of the remaining parts of BR will be sold by that date, and Railtrack will be sold by spring 1997.[69] It is reasonable to assume, therefore, that with the possible exception of Railfreight Distribution (RfD) and a minority of passenger franchises, the privatisation process will be complete by the start of 1997-98.

41. We have therefore attempted to assess the support available for passenger services in that year. Figure 2 below (which is at 1994-95 prices) has been prepared on the following assumptions[70]:

(a) The privatisation programme, including franchising and the sale of RfD, is complete. Union Railways and EPS have been transferred to the promoter of the Channel Tunnel Rail Link. BR has effectively ceased to trade, so there is no longer a circular cash flow (but if BR is still running a few passenger services the overall financial position is not greatly changed).

(b) Minor on-going grants for level crossings and freight support are excluded for the sake of clarity. Support for the PTEs, channelled through other departments and the rate support grant, has not been reduced in real terms compared to 1994-95 (but see Section III).

---

[67]DoT Press Notice No.121, 24 April 1995.

[68]Q627.

[69]The Secretary of State said on 8 June 1995 that privatisation was "roughly running to time" (Q760).

[70]The DoT, BR and Railtrack were given the opportunity to comment on an earlier version of this diagram. Their comments are published on pages 173 and 174 of Volume II.

(c) Passenger services are essentially unchanged. As regards the revenues and costs of the operators, we have assumed with one exception that they correspond to those predicted by BR for its TOUs in 1995-96.[71] Converted to 1994-95 prices, revenue from passengers in 1997-98 is therefore £2,475m, train leasing payments to the ROSCOs are £775m, and "all other costs including profit" amount to £1,650m. The exception is Railtrack's track charges, which reduce by 4% to £1,810m in line with the Regulator's decision of January 1995. On this basis, the passenger operators would require a subsidy of £1,760m.

It has been argued that franchising will release entrepreneurial talent resulting in greater efficiency and lower costs.[72] Equally, we have received evidence of costs increasing as a result of fragmentation of the railway, for example from the PTEs.[73] We have elected to take a neutral position. We present the situation as we believe it would be in 1997-98 if the current levels of costs and revenue continue unchanged in real terms from those estimated by BR for the current year. Figure 2 therefore allows the performance of franchisees to be examined against that of BR: if their subsidy requirement is less than BR's, through cost savings and revenue increases, then their requirement for funding will be lower than the sum in the diagram.

---

[71]Evidence, p.236.
[72]*New Opportunities for the Railways,* paras 19 and 21.
[73]Evidence, pp52-55.

FIGURE 2

Support for passenger services in 1997–98
(at 1994–95 prices)

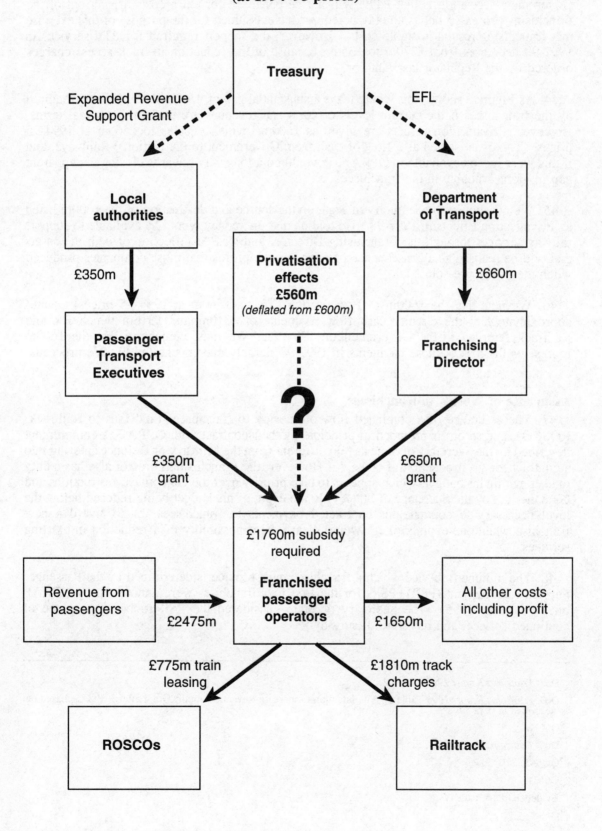

42. The Government's projected cash requirement for the national railways in 1997-98 is £670m at 1993-94 prices, say £690m at 1994-95 prices.[74] This sum embraces the EFR for BR and Railtrack which should be a few tens of millions by then, including level crossing grant at £33m for instance; Metropolitan Railway Grant which ends in March 1996 and is therefore zero; and grants to rail services by OPRAF.[75] Hence the sum available to OPRAF from the Government should be no more than £650m at best.

43. Although there is some doubt about the ability of the PTEs to sustain support for their rail services at the 1994-95 level, we have assumed that they are successful in doing so. The Government's position is that PTEs will not be penalised for extra costs arising out of the franchising process,[76] but as already noted, we have assumed for the purpose of this exercise that franchising results in stable costs. However, the support required for PTE services in 1997-98 decreases from £370m to £350m because of the reduction in track access charges ordered by the Regulator last January.

44. As Figure 2 shows, this would leave a substantial gap of £760m in the funding required by the franchisees if the current levels of costs and revenues are unchanged in real terms. However, Privatisation Effects are given as £600m[77] which equates to £560m at 1994-95 prices. This is presented as a flow of cash from Government to the National Railways, and if this were indeed available to OPRAF, it would go a long way towards closing the apparent gap in grant available to the franchisees.

45. We questioned the Secretary of State on the source and destination of the £600m listed as Privatisation Effects in 1997-98. He told us that the money would be available to support railway services through the Franchising Director, and was "a reflection of both the assets that will be realised as a consequence of sales less the profits that those companies produced when they were pre-sold."[78]

46. We note that the £600m of Privatisation Effects (£560m at 1994-95 prices) equates approximately to the circular cash flow payments of £310m and £316m which BR and Railtrack returned to the Government in 1994-95. We must conjecture that the £600m represents the loss of those payments in 1997-98, largely uncompensated by sale proceeds.

Assurance of subsidy to franchisees

47. The assurance of a continued flow of subsidy to franchisees (and thus to Railtrack, ROSCOs, and so on) is provided in principle by their contract with OPRAF, a commitment described by the Secretary of State as "no different from the Ministry of Defence entering into a contract for the production of tanks."[79] However, the Franchising Director also has a duty to keep within his budget, which appears to take priority over the Objectives, Instructions and Guidance set by the Secretary of State.[80] In the event of his budget being reduced below the level necessary to continue his contracted payments to franchisees, or to award a new franchise when one expires, there would clearly be a possibility of a reduction in existing services.

48. The minimum service which a franchisee must provide is determined by the Passenger Service Requirement (PSR). PSRs for the first four franchises were announced by OPRAF on 31 January 1995. The Secretary of State considered the PSR to be a guarantee of continued service, and therefore of subsidy.[81]

---

[74]DoT *Transport Report 1995*, Table 2.

[75]DoT *Transport Report 1995* Table 2. The intention to increase Revenue Support Grant after MRG is phased out is described in para 59.

[76]Q667.

[77]DoT *Transport Report 1995* Fig 2.

[78]QQ643, 710, 711.

[79]Q653.

[80]Evidence, p.16, para 1.2.

[81]Q638.

49. However, OPRAF advised us that the Franchising Director (as well as the franchisee) will be able to propose changes in the PSR, and that "a change procedure to allow this will be written into the franchise agreement."[82] That this poses a threat to the continuation of services is confirmed by another OPRAF statement: "If at any point in the future, the Franchising Director's budget were to be reduced to a level which was not sufficient to meet the support commitments contained within franchise agreements, then the Franchising Director would need to use this change procedure to negotiate new passenger service requirements which reflected the reduced amount of money available to support them."[83]

III LOCALLY SUPPORTED SERVICES

50. The Passenger Transport Authorities (PTAs) cover the six Metropolitan Districts of England together with the Strathclyde Region. The rail services in the PTA areas cater for twice as many passenger journeys as the former InterCity part of BR and for three quarters of those carried by the former Regional Railways.[84] The Authorities are the channel of provision of just under one fifth of the overall net subsidy required for the rail network.[85]

51. The Transport Act 1968 gave the PTAs, through their Passenger Transport Executives (PTEs), a unique role in the specification, purchase and investment in local railway services.[86] Financing of these services was arranged through what have become known as 'Section 20' agreements.[87] Until 1986 the PTAs raised the funds necessary through a direct precept by the Metropolitan Counties, or the Regional Council in the case of Strathclyde PTA.

52. The Local Government Act 1985 abolished the Metropolitan County Councils. Under the new Act the PTAs became single service authorities with the right to precept directly upon the District Councils. Central government grant towards the cost of financing local rail services and the PTAs' other services was paid directly to the PTAs. Therefore the precept levied by the PTAs only had to cover the locally funded balance of their expenditure. Subsequently, as a result of the Local Government Act 1988, the PTAs became levying bodies.[88] This meant that the PTAs had to agree with their constituent District Councils the amount of money they required to raise each year. This amount then became part of the Council Tax for each District. Central government revenue support grant (RSG) for local rail services continued but was now paid to District Councils. In consequence PTAs now have to charge the districts for their total expenditure. Individual components of RSG are not ring-fenced and therefore do not have to be passed on to PTAs. The levies of the six English PTAs totalled £456m in 1993-94 and in 1995-96 are planned to have risen to £479m, an increase over two years of 5%. The rail element of these levies, which includes all transport services including buses, remains constant at about 24%.[89]

53. The new arrangements for funding the railways which came into being with the Railways Act 1993 mean that the charges to be met by the PTAs must reflect the new costing structure of the railway industry. This requires that charges for the use of track and rolling stock now reflect modern equivalent asset value including a rate of return on assets.[90] The PTEs purchase train services from the TOUs, who in turn pay Railtrack for infrastructure services and the ROSCOs for rolling stock. Access charges increased more significantly for the PTEs in 1994-95 than for the railway industry as a whole because previously some PTE

[82]Evidence, p.122.

[83]Evidence, p.123.

[84]Evidence, p.44.

[85]Evidence, pp.4-7.

[86]Evidence, p.226.

[87]Section 20 of the Transport Act 1968; Evidence, p.44.

[88]Q250 [The change of PTAs from precepting bodies to levying bodies was included as an amendment to the Act].

[89]Q551.

[90]QQ259,262,654.

services had only met the marginal or incremental costs of infrastructure shared with other services.[91]

54. The effect of the new financing regime has therefore been to increase the financial demands upon the PTAs. It was estimated by the PTE Group that the net cost of Section 20 support, under the previous methodology, would have been £131m for the seven PTEs in the year 1994-95. Taking into account the new charging principles that were introduced from 1st April 1994, the PTEs estimated that the cost of supporting rail services would be £356m. This increase of £225m was estimated to be made up as follows:

Railtrack charges to TOUs	£141m
Rolling Stock charges to TOUs	60m
Other TOU costs	24m
	£225m[92]

55. The Director General of Strathclyde PTE told us that the local authorities were being charged for access to the track on the basis of the time the trains which they supported occupied the track. Because local trains were slower and called at more stations and there were more of them, this resulted in PTEs being asked to pay a high proportion of total costs. As more track damage was caused by the heavier, faster trains, which were run particularly by the InterCity TOUs, he did not feel that the PTEs were receiving value for money.[93]

56. It was recognised by the Government that the change brought about by the Railways Act would cause the costs to be borne by the PTEs to rise significantly. Assurances were given in 1993 by the then Minister for Public Transport to the PTE Group that special grants would be made to cover the additional costs falling to the six English PTEs in 1994-95 as a result of restructuring of the railway and the introduction of the new track and rolling stock charging system. It was made clear, in a letter, that this grant would cover the difference in agreed costs and would fall outside the District Councils' budget requirements so as not to affect the capping regime. Similar protection was promised for Scotland.[94]

57. This new grant, designated Metropolitan Railway Grant (MRG), is paid directly to the PTEs from the DoT. It was agreed originally that this would be paid in 1994-95, when it was estimated to have amounted to £146m in England and £78m in Scotland, subsequently revised downwards by £2m to give a total of £222m. MRG has now been extended to 31 March 1996.[95]

58. That part of the support for passenger railway services specified by the PTEs which does not at present flow through the MRG is funded by a mechanism known as the 'Standard Spending Assessment (SSA) bolt-on'. This part of the SSA, which is included with the 'other services' block grant, includes funding for about 31 different services.[96] The formula for calculating the railway part of the SSA is unique, in that no precise detail is made public about the way it is made up. Evidence submitted to the Committee suggested that the information used to determine the amount of the 'bolt-on' had been provided in the past by British Rail,[97] but that this information would not be available given the railways' new cost structure.[98] Despite the recommendations of the House of Commons Environment Committee on SSAs in 1994 that the process had to be made as effective, objective and transparent as possible, and that the data put into the system had to be as up-to-date and

---

[91]Evidence, p.188; Q262.

[92]Evidence, p.45.

[93]Q262.

[94]Letter from Roger Freeman MP to Councillor Mark Dowd, Chairman of PTE Group (30th September 1993); Q213.

[95]Evidence, p.6; Annex B5, *Official Report*, 31 March 1995, col 829; Evidence, p.224; *Official Report*, 14 June 1995, col 531.

[96]Q587. Examples of these services are concessionary fares, museums and galleries and civil defence.

[97]Evidence, p.225.

[98]Evidence, p.224.

accurate as possible,[99] this transparency does not seem to have applied to the 'Section 20 bolt-on'. We were told by PTA representatives that the money involved was allocated on the basis of a combination of route-miles and infrastructure costs, that the data involved were not divulged, and that the information base was flawed.[100]

TABLE 3[101]

Government support to the Railways
PTE Support 1985-86—1995-96

| | England/Wales | | | Scotland | | |
| | S20 Bolt-on | | MRG | S20 Bolt-on | | MRG |
	£ million cash	£ million 94-95 prices	£ million cash	£ million cash	£ million 94-95 prices	£ million cash
1985-86	56.2	87.3		28.5	44.3	
1986-87	59.7	90.1		30	45.3	
1987-88	67.1	96.1		30	43.0	
1988-89	62.7	84.2		30.9	41.5	
1989-90	70.1	88.0		31.1	39.0	
1990-91	77	89.5		33	38.3	
1991-92	93	101.7		35.5	38.8	
1992-93	105	110.4		34.2	36.0	
1993-94	110	112.2		32.6	33.3	
1994-95	112.9	112.9	146[1]	35.2	35.2	78[1]
1995-96[2]	112.9			34.3		

Notes:
1. Estimates.
2. Cash figures.
3. Some Shire councils have supported rail services in the past using powers in the Transport Act 1985. The sums involved are very small and are not included in the table.

59. In contrast, the Secretary of State professed keenness "to secure a formula for future funding that is both transparent and able to deliver to the PTEs the extra costs of privatisation", and was minded to revert to channelling all support for PTE rail services through an enhanced Revenue Support Grant (RSG) 'bolt-on'. The Secretary of State said that this would preserve the element of local flexibility inherent in the RSG system.[102] The Department submitted a consultation paper on the draft formula for distributing the new RSG to the Department of Environment/Local Authorities Associations SSA Sub-Group on 27 March 1995.

60. At the time they gave evidence the Committee was told by local authorities that their principal concern about the proposed future funding mechanism was that only 76.53% of every pound of SSA was met by central Government through a combination of the RSG and Non Domestic Rates, and that raising the SSA by the full amount of the MRG would therefore still leave 23.47p in each pound to be found from the local council taxpayers unless the new SSA were factored upwards to cover this gap.[103]

61. However in a letter to Councillor Dowd of the AMA the Minister for Roads and Railways, Mr John Watts MP, said that

[99]Environment Committee: First Report, HC (1993-94) 90, *Standard Spending Assessments*, paras 20 & 64.
[100]Q587.
[101]Evidence, p.6, Annex B5.
[102]Evidence, p.224.
[103]Evidence, p.225.

"although in OVERALL terms central Government funding represents 77% of Standard Spending Assessments resources this is not the basis on which RSG is provided to individual authorities. RSG is an equalising grant and compensates in full for differences in SSAs. The 'bolt-on' acknowledges additional spending needs faced by metropolitan districts providing heavy rail services through PTEs. These are not faced by other councils and are matched 100% by RSG so that those councils which face these additional needs can set council taxes at the same levels as elsewhere. You will understand that I cannot say at this stage precisely how much support will be made available through the enhanced bolt-on in 1996-97. But I expect the total level of support to continue at broadly the same level as the combination of the existing bolt-on and MRG. So, to the extent that the Government provides 100% of resources needed for PTE services now, my intention is that this will continue in future and, as I said at the meeting, my aim is to ensure that no additional burden falls on District Councils or Council taxpayers."[104]

Provided that the capping level for each District is adjusted appropriately, it therefore appears that the neccessary funds will indeed be available for the District Councils to pass on to the PTAs.

62. The Director of Finance of the South Yorkshire PTE told the Committee that there was "absolutely no commitment anywhere that the money incorporated into the Revenue Support Grant — what is referred to at present as the Section 20 bolt on — should be directly allocated and paid over to public passenger transport through the Passenger Transport Executives and Authorities."[105] Indeed the Government made a virtue of this situation in a note submitted to the Committee on 9 March 1995, as it "sets much importance by local authorities retaining local discretion so that they have the freedom to determine their own priorities".[106]

63. PTEs also expressed concern that agreement would also need to be reached between the constituent authorities about the amount of the levy. As Districts benefit to varying extents from rail services, unless formulae for grant distribution reflected those benefits accurately there would be the possibility that some Districts which received proportionately fewer benefits from railway services than others would argue that not all funds should be spent in this way. If one District argued for a reduced levy this might set the norm for other contributions.[107]

64. PTEs in the past were able to influence cash flow from year to year by deferral of maintenance or renewal of infrastructure and rolling stock. This allowed flexibility in cash flow management so that costs could be reduced in the short term if revenue fell. Under the new contractual arrangements the PTEs told us that such flexibility would no longer exist.[108]

65. Another point of concern was that if economies in rail services were needed the high proportion of fixed costs borne by the TOUs under the new system would mean substantial reductions in services to achieve relatively small financial benefits.[109] Similarly, if fares were raised by anything significantly more than inflation, consumer resistance was such that a stage of diminishing returns would quickly be reached.[110] In this connection the PTE Group said that it was essential that both Railtrack and the ROSCOs urgently improved their accounting and management regimes to ensure that 'what if' calculations could be carried out in response to possible service and other changes which might be put forward by the PTEs. This was not only to ensure greater value for money but also to estimate costs of developments or retrenchments in railway support.[111]

---

[104]Letter from Mr John Watts MP to Councillor Dowd, AMA 9 May 1995.

[105]Q217.

[106]Evidence, p.173.

[107]Q240.

[108]QQ222, 249.

[109]Q591.

[110]QQ225, 249.

[111]Evidence, p.46, answer to Question 4.

66. The PTAs told us that they would be inhibited from becoming parties to Franchise Agreements stretching beyond the period covered by secure sources of revenue funding. The Director General of Strathclyde PTE said that "unless we have a reasonable assurance that we are going to continue to subsidise the services using these facilities, we are not really going to go forward and invest in something that would give us loan debt liability for many years to come".[112] If franchise commitments for seven years or more were to be entered into, assurances about sources of funding for both revenue and capital purposes would be required for the full period of the franchise.[113]

67. Concern was also expressed by the PTEs that an investment decision, such as an electrification scheme which previously involved BR and the DoT, might now involve several more agencies and businesses, particularly if a transfer of rolling stock between services on other parts of the network were involved.[114]

68. Witnesses from the PTAs and PTEs drew attention to the rise in the costs quoted by Railtrack for new works. These were very significant;[115] one witness referred to increases being up to twofold and another complained of "a quite excessive rate of fees being put in by Railtrack for design and supervision costs".[116] The PTEs also believed that they were now funding a much larger proportion of Railtrack's central administration costs than had previously been the case,[117] and that Railtrack was not exploiting economies of scale.[118] Councillor Lyons of West Yorkshire PTA complained that Railtrack was not responding to requests for information about future charges which was required in order to make a bid for European funding.[119]

69. However, Railtrack said "we have tried hard — as the PTEs acknowledge — to provide more realistic cost estimates than they had previously been given. Many of the alleged cost increases that have taken place are also due to changes in the specification of projects."[120] It replied to PTEs that among other things:

  (a) ownership of standard BR designs remained with the BRB, and that access to these was not always available and cost money: these costs should reduce when Railtrack had its own standard designs;
  (b) project management had taken on a higher profile with Railtrack, and that PTEs were bearing an equitable share of costs;
  (c) Railtrack was aiming to obtain fixed price tenders for design and development from third parties; and
  (d) Railtrack's costs were subject to audit.[121]

70. We were told that PTAs were obliged to give BR ten months' notice of an intention to withdraw financial support from any railway service.[122] It was not clear whether this was a matter of contract law or of operational necessity, but the need to draw up timetables in areas of complex operation requires several months' notice. Witnesses also said that they had been told that if they gave notice to terminate railway services, the PTEs would not be able to take part in Section 20 arrangements and the running of these services ever again.[123]

---

[112]Q265.
[113]Q213.
[114]QQ213,265.
[115]QQ253, 271, 551.
[116]Q272.
[117]Q271
[118]Q272
[119]Q561.
[120]Evidence, p.189.
[121]Evidence, p.190.
[122]QQ214, 551, 620.
[123]QQ551, 556, 567, 615.

71. The Secretary for State told the Committee that if the PTAs gave notice not to continue to support local railway services it did not mean the services would stop: "They [the PTAs] are not the provider of operations, they are the purchasers of operations and if they decide, to my regret, not to be the purchaser of operations, then the legal framework is quite clear: the Franchising Director can take over the purchasing operation and the services will continue".[124]

72. The Secretary of State said that, exceptionally, the PTEs would be compensated to the tune of £7m for losses arising from the Railtrack strikes in 1994.[125] The PTEs would also be compensated for past investment by means of an Assumption Deed which was made when Railtrack was divorced from British Rail. This would ensure that the PTEs did not pay more than once for that investment "bearing in mind they will be meeting with their subsidies the replacement costs levied in access charges and leasing arrangements". The total written down value on which payments under the Assumption Deed were calculated was £387.2m.[126]

IV FREIGHT

73. Rail freight has been declining both absolutely and in terms of market share since the 1950s. Volume was reasonably stable throughout the 1980s with around 140 million tonnes carried and 16 billion tonne-km of freight hauled annually, but the 1990s have seen another sharp decline. Only 103 million tonnes were carried in 1993-94 generating 13.8 billion tonne-km.[127] Coal has always been the principal commodity moved by rail in Britain, and the freedom of privatised electricity generators to import coal or burn gas has cut drastically the tonnage moved by rail.[128]

74. Until 31 March 1994, there were two freight divisions within BR: Trainload Freight and Railfreight Distribution (RfD). Trainload Freight concentrated on moving complete trains of bulk commodities such as coal, stone and oil products between industrial plants or distribution centres. This business has been consistently profitable, despite the recent loss of coal tonnage, producing an operating profit of £85m despite a reduced turnover of £432m in 1993-94.[129]

75. RfD handled all those commodities which were not offered as complete trainloads, and some non-bulk products such as new cars which were. Traditional dispatch of single wagons to any rail terminal or siding on the network finally disappeared so far as domestic customers were concerned in 1991, although a limited wagonload service for international traffic continues. RfD also operated dedicated container trains under the Freightliner brand name; although the rail movements were internal, most of the containers were carried to or from ports. RfD has been loss-making for many years; in 1993-94 the operating loss was £62m compared with gross revenues of £159m.[130]

76. On 1 April 1994, Trainload was split into three competing companies which are to be sold in 1995. RfD will continue in the public sector until the pattern of Channel Tunnel traffic is established, but unsuccessful attempts were made last year to find a buyer for Freightliner, which is currently being split off from RfD so that another attempt to sell the business can be made this year.[131] Since April 1994, it has been possible for private companies to enter the freight business under the open access provisions of the Railways Act 1993, although lack of available locomotives has made this difficult.

---

[124]Q659.

[125]Q666

[126]Evidence, p 45, para 2, p52, Appendix 7.

[127]BR annual reports.

[128]Evidence, p.11, para 9.

[129]BR annual report 1993-94.

[130]ibid.

[131]Financial Times 5 January 1995.

77. In addition to the loss of tonnage since 1990, BR has reported downward pressure on rates in the more competitive coal market. Thus income from coal dropped 42% from £361m in 1990-91 to an estimated £209m for 1994-95. Worse, a further 30% drop in coal revenue is anticipated in 1995-96, "virtually all the result of price reductions due to new competitive pressure".[132]

78. BR has invested over £400m in locomotives, wagons and other works in setting up new trainload and combined transport (containers and road-rail swap bodies) services through the Channel Tunnel. Services commenced on 1 June 1994. The objective is to operate 27 freight trains a day each way through the Channel Tunnel by the end of 1995 and to carry 6 million tonnes annually in the next few years.[133] At present 100 freight trains a week are passing through the Tunnel.

79. The Government started to make grants available to rail freight customers for the provision of sidings and mechanised handling in 1975.[134] Since then, around 150 grants totalling £100m have been awarded.[135] Following the Railways Act 1993 two separate freight grants have been available. Freight Facilities Grant continues the grant system available under the 1974 Act but extends it to freight *operators*, including those remaining in BR ownership, while Track Access Grants allow the Government to subsidise up to 100% of Railtrack's charges. The intention of the grants is "to encourage freight traffic off the roads and onto the rail network",[136] but this benefit has to be demonstrated in each case which has sometimes proved difficult.[137]

80. Take-up of the 1974 grant has been poor in recent years, averaging £2.1m over the five years to 31 March 1994 at 1994-95 prices.[138] The amount allocated for the two new grants in 1994-95 was £13.3m, rising to £15.3m in 1996-97, but £5.8m of this was surrendered when the Spring Supplementary Estimates were presented to Parliament on 16 February 1995. The Secretary of State said on 15 March that no Track Access Grants had yet been awarded but that there were 11 pending.[139] On 8 June, he confirmed that the situation was unchanged, because bidders were still seeking some of the information on which to base their applications for grants, but that he wanted them to be made as quickly as possible.[140]

81. The Secretary of State has identified "longer-distance, low-volume, high value goods traffic which is currently almost the sole preserve of road" as "the kind of traffic that rail must capture if it is to reverse its long-term decline".[141] Unfortunately, there appear to be barriers to the entry of open access freight operators. Apart from the non-availability of suitable locomotives and rolling stock even small scale operators are required by the Regulator to have liability insurance cover of £155m for a single incident. This, the Department told us, was a judgement reached by the Regulator on the basis of an assessment of industry risk and historic experience. BR had been operating on the basis that £155m was "an appropriate level of cover", it added.[142] As a result of this decision the Rail Freight Group said that "premiums in excess of £100,000 [a year] have been quoted for even the most limited freight operations" even though "in BR's history no freight accident has cost more than £10m".[143]

---

[132]Evidence, p.11, paras 8-10.

[133]*A New Era Dawns*, RfD brochure, 1994.

[134]Railways Act 1974.

[135]Q685.

[136]Evidence, p.6, Annex B4 Footnote 2.

[137]A benefit is attributed to each lorry-mile directed from rural single carriageway roads (£1.50), urban single carriageway roads (£1.00), and motorways, rural dual carriageways and urban grade separated dual carriageways (5p). However in a press notice on 9 June 1995 the RFG claimed that the Department normally used 80% of these figures as the ceiling for grants.

[138]Evidence, p.6, Annex B4.

[139]Q685.

[140]QQ765-767.

[141]Speech to Freight Transport Association, March 1 1995 (see DoT Press Notice 56).

[142]Evidence, p.234.

[143]*Rail Freight Group News*, Spring 1995.

82. In December 1994 the Regulator issued Criteria and Procedures for the approval of Freight Track Access Agreements. These state that access charges must lie between "the avoidable cost floor calculated for the freight flow in question" (continuing the principle behind marginal costing of freight track charges under the 1974 Act) and "any ceiling which the Regulator has agreed with Railtrack ... for the relevant flow". He told us that he was "requiring Railtrack to take freight provided it simply covers its avoidable costs."[144]

83. Nevertheless, actual and potential rail freight customers reported to the Freight Transport Association (FTA) their fears that "the privatisation of many parts of the railway could generate sudden price increases".[145] Since the Regulator is not prepared to allow Railtrack "to sell its track access rights at a price that does not even cover the avoidable costs of carrying that traffic",[146] operators can only offset cost increases by applying for Track Access Grant.

84. Meanwhile, the Rail Freight Group (RFG) and the FTA have both reported that continuing uncertainty over the future cost and availability of rail freight services is damaging customer confidence. RFG has described the decision to postpone the sale of Freightliner pending reorganisation and separation from RfD as "extremely damaging to prospects of retaining a national network for maritime containers ... no new contracts have been signed nor any significant new business attracted".[147] The FTA reported that "uncertainty over the future stability of rail freight rates remains a key concern acting against the use of rail for many customers".[148]

V INVESTMENT AND MAINTENANCE

Total Railway Investment

85. The Department provided the following information on investment in the existing railway and in Channel Tunnel-related schemes in recent and future years:

---

[144]Q373.

[145]*The Rail Freight Challenge*, FTA, February 1995.

[146]Q375.

[147]*Rail Freight Group News*, Spring 1995.

[148]*The Rail Freight Challenge*, FTA, February 1995, para 6.2.

TABLE 4[149]

Railway Investment 1985-86—1993-94

	Existing Railway		EPS and Channel Tunnel Freight		Total	
	£ million cash	£ million 94-95 prices	£ million cash	£ million 94-95 prices	£ million cash	£ million 94-95 prices
1985-86	550	855			550	855
1986-87	543	819			543	819
1987-88	693	993			693	993
1988-89	723	970	5	7	728	977
1989-90	865	1,085	27	34	892	1,119
1990-91	869	1,009	178	207	1,047	1,216
1991-92	969	1,059	350	383	1,319	1,442
1992-93	955	1,004	521	548	1,476	1,552
1993-94	650	663	515	525	1,165	1,188
TOTAL	6,817	8,459	1,596	1,704	8,413	10,161

FUTURE INVESTMENT PLANS

The forecast total for 1994-95 is around £1.1 billion including approximately £100 million of private finance. Investment in 1995-96 is also expected to be around £1 billion, of which around £750 million will be publicly funded and about £250 million privately financed. Figures are not available for future years when it is expected that the private sector will have taken on substantial responsibility for investment.

86. BR's investment figures show the extent to which investment has shifted from rolling stock to infrastructure in the last two years, following replacement of the ageing Regional Railways fleet and the provision of new trains in the south-east to meet the growth in commuting demand:[150]

TABLE 5[151]

Railway Investment (Excluding Channel Tunnel)

£ million	1990-91	1991-92	1992-93	1993-94	1994-95*
Rolling Stock	353	387	429	165	135
Other	660	676	579	500	480
TOTAL	1,013	1,063	1,008	665	615

* Estimated and including Railtrack

BR told us that

"With the economic recession, passenger demand fell and the need for new rolling stock diminished. It was, however, clear that increasing priority would need to be given to re-equipping the existing railway infrastructure. The Board's plans emphasised the requirement for major infrastructure renewal, including the replacement of certain major signalling installations. In its evidence to a previous Committee inquiry the Board estimated that total investment in the existing railway amounting to roundly £900m a year would be required in order to sustain the steady state. Whilst the level of expenditure may vary from that level in any one year, the Board remains of the view that broadly this

[149]Annex D, Evidence, p.8.

[150]Evidence, p.12, para 15.

[151]Table 8, Evidence, p.12.

average level of expenditure will need to be spent in order to maintain the existing system"[152]

Infrastructure investment is now in the hands of Railtrack. We were told that because of financial pressures BR would only have about £100m to spend on capital investment in 1995-96, of which £70m was already committed.[153]

Railtrack's Maintenance and Investment Programme

87. Of its £2.1 billion annual expenditure, Railtrack expects to spend about £800m per year on 'infrastructure maintenance'. Railtrack told us that

> "this heading covers not only the costs of maintaining track, signalling electrification and operational telecommunications but also structures such as bridges, tunnels, depots and stations. This level of expenditure represents a steady state maintenance cost and does not provide for any catching up of outstanding work."

Most of Railtrack's maintenance work is contracted out to the British Rail Infrastructure Service (BRIS) companies. The Government is reviewing Railtrack's contracts with the BRIS companies, which account for about 50% of Railtrack's direct operating costs.[154]

88. As regards investment in renewals, we were told that

> "Railtrack's track access contracts with its customers require it to maintain the track to a certain standard. Failure to do so would attract penalty payments. The company believes that the level of expenditure needed to achieve a steady state in which it can deliver its obligations under these contracts is broadly £600m a year."[155]

The precise level of its current cost depreciation is believed by Railtrack to be £570m per year, although the amount may differ slightly from year to year depending on asset condition. This is expenditure on renewal of assets, classified as investment, which is over and above the £800m a year required for maintenance. Maintenance expenditure would rise rapidly in the absence of adequate investment in renewals.[156]

89. In his decision on the level of Railtrack's charges, the Regulator said that he had

> "accepted Railtrack's forecast that it needs to spend on average some £570m per annum on infrastructure investment and has fully provided for this in his pricing limits. In opting to fund such expenditure through a depreciation charge rather than a 'pay as you go' basis the Regulator has relied on commitments made by the Government that it intends to continue to support the current network and timetable level of services."[157]

He would, however,

> "monitor the investment programme actually undertaken by Railtrack. Railtrack's Network Licence already requires Railtrack to provide information on its capital programme and accounting information. At the next periodic review of charges, the Regulator will want to consider, in the event of a failure to deliver the capital investment programme, whether there should be a significant reduction in prices to compensate operators."[158]

---

[152]Evidence, p.12-13, para 16.

[153]QQ107-111; Evidence, p.13, para 23.

[154]Evidence, p.20, para 16(i).

[155]Evidence, p.21, para 4.

[156]Evidence, p.20, para 16(ii).

[157]Evidence, p.23, para 11.

[158]Evidence, p.23, para 12.

The Regulator believed that Railtrack would benefit from a regulatory regime which covered its operating costs (even though it imposed tough efficiency targets), provided in full for the investment it required and provided for reasonable profit.[159]

Maintenance and Investment Levels and Equipment Orders

90. The Railway Industry Association (RIA) claimed that "the slow pace of privatisation, and the uncertainties surrounding the process, are delaying essential renewal of the system". This would have serious consequences for the whole of the railway supply industry, and the Association was not optimistic that the situation would improve over the next three years at least.[160] We therefore decided to seek evidence on the level of orders for railway equipment as well as the level of expenditure. We analyse below the levels of spending and equipment orders in three important areas: signalling equipment, trackwork and rolling stock.

Signalling Equipment

91. Railtrack told us that one of the key features of its investment plan was "a programme of minor signalling renewals and modernisation works. The expenditure is driven by asset condition and the need to ensure the integrity of existing systems until a major scheme can be progressed."[161] It planned to spend about £175m in 1995-96 on signalling, which compared favourably with previous years.[162] In addition, Railtrack plans to spend £130m on 'Channel Tunnel Works' which include a significant signalling component.[163]

92. These figures are higher than the spending envisaged in the Hesketh Report, a report commissioned by BR and completed in 1992. The purpose of this report was to indicate the forthcoming requirements for the renewal of signalling and associated systems throughout BR over the next 15 years. This timetable was considered appropriate because of the way in which equipment of different periods and manufacturers aged at different rates. The report "underlined the [BR] Board's determination to switch the main thrust of investment in the 1990s from traction and rolling stock into infrastructure".[164] The report listed in order of indicative priority the sites and work that it believed needed to be done, the duration of the work, and the latest start date. A summary of the report is published in Volume II of this Report and we intend to place the complete document in the Parliamentary Record Office. In the summary, BR told us that the report demonstrated a steady build up in the requirement for signalling work during the 1990s "with a peak of about £140m per annum needed in the years 1999-2004. Thereafter there was a noticeable easing of the situation with roughly £60m per annum required from 2007 onwards. In global terms some £120m per annum would be needed for re-signalling and signal renewals for the fifteen years from 1993."[165] Railtrack told us that it had updated the Hesketh Report with its consultants, and assured us that it was "spending at a level which entirely fits the sequence which both Hesketh originally proposed and we have cross-checked with independent consultants".[166]

93. We received evidence, though, which contended that Railtrack was not placing orders for signalling equipment at a level commensurate with keeping the rail network in a steady state. The RIA told us that

"Railtrack has inherited a total of some 23,000 track-miles of railway which have been starved of sustained investment for many years. The result is that the control and safety of the network is managed by a bewildering variety of equipment dating in some cases from the last century. For Railtrack to keep the network in a steady state, a rolling plan for replacement and maintenance is needed. At a cost for signalling of around £150,000

---

[159]Evidence, p.23, para 13.

[160]Evidence, pp.57&59.

[161]Evidence, p.20, para 17.

[162]QQ143-4.

[163]QQ128,152.

[164]Evidence, p.201.

[165]Evidence, p.202.

[166]Q142.

per mile, the total costs would be in the region of £3.5 billion. On the assumption that the life of equipment is about 20 years, this implies an investment of £175m per year. However, because the programme needs to catch up on past underinvestment we consider than an annual level of, say, £225m is necessary. Despite repeated references to the production of one, three and ten year investment plans by Railtrack, none have yet been published."[167]

The RIA was also able to provide figures for the aggregate turnover of the three main UK-based signalling suppliers and of other specialist equipment suppliers:

TABLE 6[168]

Signalling sector turnover with British Rail and Railtrack

£ million

1990-91	1991-92	1992-93	1993-94	1994-95*	1995-96*
39.1	47.3	50.1	58.2(a)	44.1(a)	37.6(a)

* Estimate

(a) Includes about £5.0 million in each year relating to civil engineering.

TABLE 7[169]

Calls for tender for major signalling schemes by British Rail and Railtrack

1990-91	1991-92	1992-93	1993-94	1994-95
10	5	2	2	1

94. Mr Hugh Bayley MP, the Member for York, told us that the two companies formed out of BR's Signalling Project Group — Interlogic Control Engineering and Signalling Control UK — were not receiving the orders they had expected from Railtrack and jobs were being lost as a result.[170] The Institution of Railway Signal Engineers told us that the age and safety of electrical signalling introduced in the 1950s and 1960s was causing concern: "lack of finance would appear to have delayed both renewal and improvement to these safety systems and the current indications are that this situation will worsen". The Institution was concerned that the degradation of insulating wires on some installations might result in parts of the network being closed down.[171] Transport 2000 drew attention to the reappraisal of the continuing Great Eastern resignalling programme carried out in 1994; this had delayed the work and "the Gospel Oak - Barking Line was cut out with no alternative plans proposed".[172]

95. We put the evidence we had received from the RIA and about the two successors to the BR Signalling Project Group to Railtrack. The company provided a paper which detailed the signalling schemes being undertaken in 1995-96.[173] Within this, Railtrack identified £44m spent with RIA members and a further £15m spent with external contractors. It believed that the RIA figures might also be distorted by being based on the turnover of the companies (which included an 'up front' payment of £40m to GEC Alsthom in 1993-94) and not on the

---

[167]Evidence, p.60, para 19.

[168]Table 3, Evidence, p.60.

[169]Table 4, Evidence, p.60.

[170]Evidence, p.218.

[171]Evidence, p.75.

[172]Evidence, p.200.

[173]Evidence, pp.209-211.

value of the work done. The difference between the total of £200m to be spent by Railtrack in 1995-96 and the £60m spent with contractors was due to a number of factors which included money spent within the railway industry on:

— associated civil engineering works by BRIS units and external civil engineering contractors;

— alterations to/remodelling of the permanent way;

— signalling design work by Interlogic and Signalling Control UK (obtained in general by competitive tender);

— associated BR Telecommunications work;

— major charges from the freight operating companies for the use of engineering trains; and

— Railtrack project management costs.[174]

Railtrack said that the fact that only one signalling scheme went to tender in 1994-95 was a function of the phasing of these tenders.[175]

96. As for Signalling Control UK and Interlogic Control Engineering, Railtrack told us that their speciality was in design and that therefore their work would not necessarily relate closely to the current level of contracts. Railtrack also did not believe that the companies were particularly skilled in transmission-based signalling,[176] which was the direction it wished to go in future, for example in the project to upgrade the West Coast Main Line.[177] Members of the RIA told us that although such technology was in use on self-contained metro-type railways, it was relatively new, and that while it would be possible to introduce it on a complex main line like the West Coast route, it might be ten years before it could be developed, proved and installed.[178]

Trackwork

97. Railtrack told us that its investment plan envisaged spending about £200m per year on track renewals in order to maintain the existing condition of the infrastructure.[179] In 1994-95 the level was £195m, the same as in the previous four years. The number of miles replaced would vary with the amount of work required in different cases but would be about 500 route-miles in 1994-95.[180] The total track mileage subject to temporary speed restrictions had fallen by 12% since 1992, and efforts were to be made in the next few years to reduce the restrictions on the most commercially important routes.[181] BR regarded it as 'essential' that about £200m worth of track renewals took place each year, preferably in consultation with the train operating companies.[182] Any reduction from this £200m figure would require more to be spent on maintenance.[183]

98. The RIA gave us evidence on the level of orders placed with manufacturers of trackwork:

(a) *Switches (points) and crossings.* The turnover of the relevant supplies in recent years has been, according to the RIA, as follows:

---

[174]Evidence, p.210.

[175]Q178.

[176]Transmission-based signalling avoids the use of lineside equipment and cables, replacing them with a radio data link between the train and the control centre. The train reports its position continuously, and as the control centre computer knows where all the other trains are, it can send back an instruction not to exceed a safe speed. The driver is automatically prevented from exceeding the safe speed, and thus from colliding with another train.

[177]Q143.

[178]QQ430-447.

[179]Evidence, p.20, para 17.

[180]Evidence, p.21, para 25.

[181]Evidence, pp.205 and 209.

[182]Q66.

[183]Q77.

TABLE 8[184]

Switch and crossing sector turnover with British Rail and Railtrack

£ million

1990-91	1991-92	1992-93	1993-94	1994-95*
9.4	9.8	9.6	8.7	5.5

* Estimate
Note: Estimates for 1995-96 are not available

(b) *Rails*. Information from the only UK manufacturer of rails, British Steel Track Products, was that

"in the period 1980 to 1985, British Rail replaced on average 2.1% of its running rails each year. In the period 1985 to 1990 this had dropped to 1.3% and in the latest period, from 1990 to 1995, the figure has fallen further to an average of 1.1%. Whilst some of this reduction is due to improved quality of rail, better track layouts and improved rolling stock suspension, a rail replacement rate of 1.1% would mean that rails had reached a predictable life of over 90 years. Even British Steel admit that this is not possible. Annex C is a more detailed analysis of recent years, and shows that between 1991 and 1993 the National Railways of France and Sweden replaced an average 2.7% of their rails every year whereas British Rail replaced 1.3%. Precise track mileage figures are not available for Italy and Germany but on the basis of comparative route-miles, their rail replacement rates were even higher. By 1994 British Rail's rail replacement rate had dropped still further to 0.8%. Unfortunately, 1994 information for other European Railways is not yet available."[185]

(c) *Fastenings*. Pandrol Rail Fastenings Ltd, which supplies the clips that secure rails to the sleepers, gave information that major continental European railways bought between 200 and 250 resilient fastening units per route-kilometre every year. In 1992 BR had bought 231 units per route-kilometre. However, "by 1994 purchases had dropped to 131 units which places Britain at the bottom of the European league, if Italian non-resilient purchases are included."[186]

99. We asked Railtrack to comment on these figures. We were told that while there was "undoubtedly some diminution in the extent of new point and trackwork being used", 70% of current orders for switches and crossings were being supplied from the BR depot at Baileyfields in preparation for privatisation of that facility. As far as rail and fastenings were concerned, the programme of purchases had been cut but the BR infrastructure units (BRIS) had been living heavily on their inventories in recent months. Railtrack expected that orders would soon begin to be placed again when the inventories had been exhausted.[187]

100. The RIA was not convinced that stocks within the BRIS units were large enough to enable Railtrack to change so completely its ordering pattern for equipment like Pandrol rail clips and rails, but was unable to explain why purchases of such equipment had fallen so far behind the European average.

101. The Association questioned the logic of switch and crossing orders being kept in-house rather than being placed with private industry during a privatisation process.[188] The RIA was also concerned that BRIS units were competing on favourable terms for the small amount of track renewal work that was already in the private sector. It suggested that an explanation

---

[184]Table 6, Evidence, p.61.

[185]*Ibid* and Annex C, Evidence, p.66.

[186]Evidence, p.61 and Annexes D and E, Evidence, pp67-8.

[187]Q141.

[188]QQ458-9.

might be that the Government would wish to sell the units with full order books, but the Department had not replied to a letter about this matter from the Director of the RIA sent more than six months before our evidence session.[189] Nevertheless, the RIA felt that the privatisation of the BRIS units would provide the opportunity for rationalisation of the UK infrastructure maintenance industry, allowing it to compete with the largely private continental European companies in the field. RIA members would therefore be interested in purchasing the BRIS units.[190]

Rolling Stock

102. The RIA told us that the hiatus in orders was affecting the rolling stock manufacturing sector worst of all. Manufacturers of track and signalling equipment had been able to secure more orders either from UK customers other than BR and Railtrack or through exports.[191] The RIA provided the following information on recent and future rolling stock orders:

TABLE 9[192]

Rolling stock sector turnover with British Rail — excluding international Eurostar trains

£ million

1990-91	*1991-92*	*1992-93*	*1993-94*	*1994-95**	*1995-96**
348.0	417.3	292.2	276.8	253.6	145.0

* Estimate

TABLE 10[193]

Calls for tender for rolling stock by British Rail — number of vehicles by class type

1990-91	*1991-92*	*1992-93*	*1993-94*	*1994-95*
Cl. 166 *63 vehicles*	IC 250 (a)	Cl. 320/321 (a)	Cl. 465 (b) *165 vehicles*	Nil
Cl. 323 *172 vehicles*	Channel Tunnel night stock *139 vehicles*		IC 225 (a,b)	
Cl. 465 *188 vehicles*			Cl. 157 (c)	
Cl. 466 *86 vehicles*				

(a) No order placed
(b) £150 million leasing deal
(c) Order placed but not proceeded with

103. Several witnesses called attention to a particular recent episode, the decision by BR in January 1995 not to order the fourth tranche of Networker trains on a leased basis for its South Eastern routes.[194] This would mean that the current 'slam door' stock on these lines would not be replaced until 1999 at the earliest. It was put to us by York City Council that

---

[189]QQ459-461, 464.

[190]QQ463-466.

[191]Q457.

[192]Table 1, Evidence p.59.

[193]Table 2, Evidence, p.60.

[194]The 'Networker' suburban train has been manufactured both by GEC Alsthom and ABB.

failing to replace the trains would mean that passengers would be deprived of improvements in comfort, reliability and safety.[195]

104. BR told us that to have ordered the trains would have worsened the financial position of its TOU in Kent, but that it was still negotiating with the manufacturers of Networkers to see if the price could be reduced. It would also be necessary to ensure that the order satisfied the requirements of the Government's Private Finance Initiative, because the priority for spending under the National Railway's EFL was the infrastructure (owing to the amount which had been spent on rolling stock in recent years).[196] This point was also made by the Secretary of State.[197] He was able to tell us that BR would 'very soon' invite tenders for up to 40 Networkers, and this was indeed announced on 21 March. The contract would have to be competitively tendered, and funding would be provided from the private sector.[198] BR told us that although GEC Alsthom and ABB both replied to this invitation to tender for these trains, neither company complied with the terms of the tender.[199]

105. The prospect of this order was not enough to prevent significant job losses. ABB told us that it had 1,800 jobs at risk, including 750 at its York factory.[200] Orders of about £300-350m per year were necessary to retain these employees, and this was unlikely, with no work forecast beyond 1995 apart from the possibility of the 40 new trains.[201] On 11 May 1995 ABB in fact announced that its York works would close by the end of 1995.

106. GEC believed that its situation was rather better, chiefly because of its success in developing its export markets, but although it felt able to cope with a hiatus in orders, it would not be able to cope with a complete cessation of orders.[202] Mr Harman and Professor Atkin believed that 40 trains needed to be ordered every year for the next 20 years. Without such investment the railways would deter custom by presenting an impression of an ageing system.[203]

107. GEC did not believe that there would be any large scale acquisition of new rolling stock until the train operating companies were securely established.[204] It identified the Franchising Director, as the source of subsidies for the operating companies, as having a central role in the encouragement of the supply of new rolling stock through leasing.[205] The RIA also believed that OPRAF's decisions on service levels would affect the size of rolling stock fleets.[206] BR pointed out that the rolling stock market would not be regulated after privatisation and that the decisions whether to order new rolling stock would lie with the ROSCOs.[207] The Franchising Director explained that until franchises were let, the responsibility for ordering rolling stock remained with BR. He told us that he expected that potential franchisees who wished to bid on the basis of operating new rolling stock could negotiate simultaneously with the Franchising Director and the rolling stock suppliers.[208]

108. The PTEs argued that the practice of 'cascading' rolling stock from one area to another as new trains were introduced would be problematic under the new arrangements: "... some of the benefits accrue to the train operating company and therefore back to OPRAF or

---

[195]Evidence, pp.69-74.

[196]QQ19-24, Q70.

[197]Q707.

[198]QQ704-6; BR press release, 21 March 1995.

[199]Evidence, p.236.

[200]Q521.

[201]QQ538,517.

[202]QQ490-1.

[203]Evidence, p.77.

[204]Q486.

[205]Q488.

[206]Evidence, p.63.

[207]QQ57,68.

[208]Q332.

ourselves, some may accrue to the rolling stock companies or the cost may lie there, some may lie with Railtrack and quite frankly we have not yet found a way through that jungle".[209] The Franchising Director believed that cascading would still work, although it would involve "a more elaborate negotiation".[210]

Major Projects

109. Railtrack's investment plan included the modernisation of the West Coast Main Line (WCML). A feasibility study had been completed and was being discussed with Government, OPRAF and train operators. The project would be the most important undertaken by the railways since the modernisation of the East Coast Main Line in 1984-91, and it was hoped that work would begin in the 1995-96 financial year.[211] Railtrack also said that it was keen to start work on major enhancements to the network, such as the Thameslink 2000 scheme to improve rail services from north to south across London, "provided that these can be economically justified".[212]

110. On the other hand, the RIA said that

"The West Coast Line is an important example of how the combination of the privatisation process, the restricted level of public investment and the insistence on the role of the private finance initiative is causing delay to a major renewal project that is widely recognised as essential and long overdue. In fact tenders were invited for new IC250 [250 km/h] trains, but their procurement was aborted in August 1992. New trains for this route will not now be ordered until there is agreement on a private sector sponsored project to renew the route's infrastructure. The new trains are likely to be provided under a design, build, finance, operate and maintain project which would require a franchise agreement of at least 20 years. Such a franchise is unlikely to be granted until 1997 at the earliest."[213]

111. The Franchising Director told us that

"The position on franchising the InterCity West Coast (ICWC) franchise is as announced by me on 14 December 1994, namely that I invited expressions of interest from potential bidders in the expectation of issuing tenders for ICWC during 1995. The comprehensive programme of infrastructure modernisation required on the WCML distinguishes it from other franchises. Before issuing a pre-qualification document, I wish to solicit views from prospective franchisees as to what form of modernisation programme they would like to see and consequently what form of franchise might be appropriate. I have stated that I would be willing to consider proposals from potential franchisees which involve enhancements directed towards improving the standard of service on a commercial basis, perhaps coupled with a longer franchise term. These enhancements would require increased track access charges which would be payable by franchisees. I anticipate that prospective franchisees would work with Railtrack in the specification of the modernisation programme."[214]

The Private Finance Initiative

112. The Private Finance Initiative (PFI) was launched in 1992 in order to "find new ways of mobilising the resources of the private sector to meet the needs which have traditionally been met only by the public sector."[215] While welcoming the PFI, the RIA was concerned that the speed at which projects were being brought forward was "painfully slow". All public sector investment projects now had to be tested against the PFI, and unless the PFI test

---

[209]Q265.

[210]Q335.

[211]Evidence, p.21, para 17; QQ157-8.

[212]Evidence, p.21, para 18.

[213]Evidence, p.59, para 16.

[214]Evidence, p.18, para 3.2.

[215]Autumn Statement 1992, para 2.111.

analysis and decision making elements of a project could be speeded up, there was a danger that the procurement process would be extended. The Association was also worried that major renewal projects which did not produce a return adequate for the private sector, but which were necessary to maintain the railway in a steady state, would not attract funding.[216] The Institution of Civil Engineers was also concerned that the PFI might delay much-needed investment projects.[217] GEC Alsthom, on the other hand, while admitting that investment *via* the PFI would probably take longer at first, thought that once the system became more routine there might not necessarily be any delay as a result of the mechanism. It said that BR had itself been slow in evaluating tenders and placing orders, and that, even though the PFI made procurement more complex, in the future orders might be placed more quickly.[218] Transport 2000 believed that private finance was unlikely to be available for "relatively small local or regional schemes".[219]

VI THE PROSPECTS FOR EFFICIENCY AND REVENUE IMPROVEMENT

Changes arising from Restructuring

113. The Secretary of State said he believed that to halt the relative decline of the railways structural change would be required. He said that "In the other privatisations we have put in private finance, private investment decisions, private management skills, and the private sector sensitivity to what the customer wants and that has produced the sort of change with which all of us are familiar".[220] However, Sir Bob Reid said that moving to a contractual rather than a command structure was potentially problematic in that in the former managers had 'alibis' whereas in the latter a manager had total responsibility for the services in his area.[221]

114. The Secretary of State told us that services over and above the Passenger Service Requirements (PSRs) would be at marginal cost and it would consequently be in operators' interests to run them. He added that "those who are operating on the commercially known viable lines will know that the subsidy from the Franchising Director enables them to continue to offer services without the sort of pressure which has been applied to British Rail on a number of occasions over the years which has actually helped them to reduce and sometimes to stop providing services on some lines".[222] The Office of the Rail Regulator (ORR) told us that the Regulator wished to see greater flexibility and variability of charging structures in future, leading to "trading of capacity at the margin, based on its value to operators and to Railtrack", in the hope that "these developments will help operators to make better use of capacity and to relate the costs of capacity more closely to service provision".[223]

115. We were told that contracts formed with the new franchisees would not be invariable over the life of the franchise. Railtrack told us that the Regulator had said that there would be scope to vary contracts from their initial terms and so there would be a process by which charges could be adjusted according to changes which the train operator wished to make.[224] The Franchising Director said that the Secretary of State had asked him to set up franchises "so that there will be gradual change in services provided to reflect customer demand" and that the PSRs issued to date had been designed to that end. He said he was "aiming for progressive improvement in the standards of service".[225]

---

[216]Evidence, p.62, paras 24-27.

[217]Evidence, p.222, para 6.

[218]Q493.

[219]Evidence, p.196.

[220]Q672.

[221]Q13.

[222]Q638

[223]Evidence, p22, para 8.

[224]Q146

[225]Q279

The Prospect of Efficiency Gains

116. BR said that "some reduction in Railtrack costs had been determined by the Regulator, and the downward pressure on operating costs by the TOUs will continue".[226] However, BR warned that while the franchisees' operating costs might be reduced through greater efficiency, given the improvements in productivity over the last five years, "the scope for substantial reduction in the short term may be limited".[227] BR estimated that it had reduced its own costs by about 4% over the previous year.[228] Railtrack told us that its own costs were approximately £400m a year, mainly signalling and train control, and that future savings in these costs would come from investment in new signalling and control systems and from computing systems which were being developed.[229] However, OPRAF cautioned that "Short-term options for controlling the cost of passenger rail services tend to achieve savings at a disproportionate cost to quality", which would be incompatible with the statutory objectives of the Franchising Director.[230]

117. Railtrack said that because of the level at which access charges had been set by the Regulator, substantial efficiency improvements would be required. Achieving these would be an "exceptionally challenging task" but Railtrack was determined to do so.[231] In oral evidence Mr Horton told us that Railtrack was "very much in the middle of working out how we achieve that and whether indeed we can, because of course if we do not, we will not make an operating profit in our first year".[232] However, as noted in paragraph 34 of this report, the amount of profit which Railtrack must remit to Government in 1995-96 has been reduced to compensate for the lower access charges. Mr Horton added that he could not make any profit forecast until the prospectus for privatisation was published.[233]

118. Mr Horton said further that because approximately 70% of Railtrack's costs were in other people's hands [the costs of maintaining and renewing the infrastructure which Railtrack had placed with contractors, eg the BRIS companies] "we cannot be expected to achieve the reduction in our total overall bill unless we expect that to be passed on to other people".[234] The ORR told us that while Railtrack remained in the public sector, altering the level of its charges had no effect on the industry EFL because there was a "parallel and equivalent" alteration in the Franchising Director's subsidy requirement.[235] BR expected Railtrack's reduction in access charges to lead to a £1 for £1 reduction in the level of subsidy available to the industry.[236]

119. Mr Horton told us that when the Regulator ended his restriction on open access in 2001 greater traffic levels would be achievable which would be "highly desirable" and would enable Railtrack to lower charges where there was greater competition.[237] Railtrack told us that it would compensate train operators under the access contracts "if its performance falls below the benchmarks established in the contracts". Whether this was passed on to PTEs in areas where they supported services was a matter for the relevant PTEs and train operators.[238] The Regulator told us he was "hopeful" that any lowering of access charges by Railtrack would benefit the passenger but could not ensure that the franchisees' shareholders would not be the sole beneficiaries: "I am hopeful it will be seen that when Railtrack ultimately serves the interests of the passengers, that the savings which are passed

[226]Evidence, p.212.

[227]Evidence, p.174.

[228]Evidence, p.12, para 13.

[229]Evidence, p20, para 16iii.

[230]Evidence, p17, para 1.7.

[231]Evidence, p19, para 5.

[232]Q136

[233]Q198

[234]Q194

[235]Evidence, p.23, para 10.

[236]Q50.

[237]QQ205-6

[238]Evidence, p.189, para 6.

on to the train operators and which could... be taken and put into the Franchising Director's pocket, will find their way through to the passengers, but on that point... I can exhort but I cannot command."[239]

120. BR said that almost £400m of its Treasury contribution target for 1995-96 would be financed from increased receipts and reductions in investment (which was mainly on rolling stock in 1994-95), with the remainder being sought from cost reductions and working capital improvements. BR believed it would be able to offer a service "broadly comparable" with the current timetable.[240] However, Sir Bob Reid cautioned that as a result of productivity gains which had already been made in the industry, "when you are looking for ways of balancing the books in the future, productivity may make a contribution, but it will become increasingly marginal". He said that this was "a warning signal that we have put out quite strongly".[241] DoT officials, however, told us that "Ministers would consider pessimistic an assumption that there is no improvement, either in operating costs or revenue performance, over the next three years".[242]

Prospects for Revenue Generation

121. OPRAF told us that its aim was "to exercise control over the general level of regulated fares whilst allowing scope for changes to specific fares which will enable franchisees to correct any anomalies and respond to market changes and opportunities within limits which protect the interests of individual passengers".[243] It would regulate fares "only where this is necessary to protect passengers from possible excessive increases made where the franchisee had a monopoly on service provision and where competition with other modes of transport could not be expected to provide effective protection for passengers". Examples given by OPRAF included season tickets, particularly into Greater London, where commuters had few realistic alternatives to rail travel, and standard single tickets in areas where a high proportion of those purchasing such tickets were commuters.[244]

122. The fares regulation regime acutally announced by OPRAF on 15 May cast the net wider than this, covering most lines and not just those used by commuters. Saver fares, unrestricted Standard returns where there are no Savers, and Standard weekly seasons must not increase by more than the Retail Price Index for three years from January 1996, or by 1% less than RPI (RPI-1%) in each of the four years thereafter. Around London, Edinburgh and Cardiff, where there is significant commuting, all Standard seasons, singles and unrestricted returns are covered. There is scope for rises up to RPI+2% on individual fares and where service quality has improved, but OPRAF reserves the right to penalise operators for poor service by imposing an RPI-2% cap. Commenting on the new policy, the Secretary of State for Transport said that "in the last 10 years fares have risen 22% above inflation. Now passengers can look forward to enjoying a period of stability and then a real fall in many rail fares".[245] The policy would ensure that efficiency gains from privatisation would be shared between passengers and private sector operators.[246]

123. Fares controlled by the PTEs are excluded from this regime. However, the PTEs had already told us that they were marketing their rail services to the best of their ability in order to attract more travellers to the railways and were very cautious about imposing fare increases above inflation because this would impact on the very people they were trying to entice onto the service. They also referred to the sensitivity of passengers to fare increases[247]. They felt too that they had been hampered by service unreliability arising both from the industrial

---

[239]Q363

[240]Evidence, p13, para 23.

[241]Q79.

[242]Evidence, p.173.

[243]Evidence, p120, para 4.1.

[244]Evidence, p120, para 2; Q180.

[245]OPRAF/DoT joint press notice, 15 May 1995; Evidence, p.232-234.

[246]QQ739-740.

[247]QQ225,249.

action of 1994 and from the introduction of new rolling stock.[248] BR agreed that, apart from commuter fares likely to be controlled by OPRAF, there was little scope for real price increases which were in any case contrary to PTE policy. There had been no significant real increase in InterCity and Regional Railways fares for some time, reflecting demand elasticity in that market.[249]

124. BR told us that when Railtrack was created, "operational" property passed to the new organisation, while "non-operational" property remained with BR. Operational property is "land supporting tracks, stations and other structures required for the operation of the railway". BR was required to dispose of its surplus property as quickly as possible, while the income from the remainder (currently around £16m a year) would be used to pay for continuing liabilities, such as maintenance of bridges on redundant branch lines.[250]

125. BR reported that passenger revenue had already recovered to pre-strike levels.[251] However, demand for passenger services, and hence revenue, is sensitive to economic activity. BR told us that in the years of recession between 1990-91 and 1993-94 real income from the former InterCity and Network SouthEast services fell by 13% and 4% respectively. Further, BR told us that "the economic recovery has taken a considerable time to feed through into passenger income...". These factors, and the impact of industrial action in 1994 on revenue levels, made revenue forecasts for future years "subject to considerable uncertainty".[252]

126. Railtrack said that over 80% of its forecast income of £2.4 billion in 1994-95 would come from access charges and that the Regulator's conclusions on competition policy meant that "competition from open access passenger operators will not represent a significant source of income in the first five years". It would be hard to increase income from freight traffic and while it would attempt to maximise its property income, the Regulator had indicated that income from property up to the level currently estimated to be achievable should all be ploughed back into reducing access charges. Income in excess of currently predicted levels would be shared between the company and train operators according to a formula decided by the Regulator.[253] However, Railtrack told us that the retail opportunities at stations were "quite considerable", as had been demonstrated at Victoria and Liverpool Street stations in London.[254]

127. ABB said that the price of rolling stock worldwide had fallen sharply and GEC Alsthom told us that they expected the price of rolling stock to decrease in real terms over the next 10 years.[255] This might give train operators scope to cut costs or raise profit margins.

128. Transport 2000 drew attention to the steep increase in the capital costs of new trains which appeared to have resulted from the privatisation of the design process, followed by the move into leasing. Whereas electric multiple-unit trains of various classes had cost around £1.6m per four-car unit in the 1980s, the Class 465 Networkers recently supplied for Kent Link services had cost £3m per unit, at current prices, and "the latest Class 365 Networkers come out at £3.6m each although the capital cost is being borne by lessors and their financiers".[256]

---

[248]Q270.

[249]Evidence, p.212, para A5.

[250]Evidence, p. 213, para A8.

[251]Evidence, p.174; Q72.

[252]Evidence, p11, para 7.

[253]Evidence, p19, para 8; QQ191, 372.

[254]Q191

[255]QQ515, 525.

[256]Evidence, p.198.

VII PRIVATISATION COSTS

129. The Secretary of State believed that "in the medium to long-term... the consequences of rail privatisation may well have benefits to the taxpayer as well as to the customer".[257] Mr Welsby of BR said that "from the taxpayer's point of view you have essentially traded an outgoing incomes cash stream in the future against a capitalised value that you have received from the sale of the assets."[258] Sir Bob Reid added that the extent to which this would benefit the taxpayer would depend on the amount for which the assets were sold which had not yet been determined.[259] Once in the private sector, Railtrack would pay corporation tax and so would continue to contribute to Treasury funds as it had since the restructuring of the industry.[260]

130. BR agreed that "in principle the changing financial flows should make no difference to the overall call on public expenditure by the industry as long as the component parts remain within the public sector".[261] After privatisation, however, lower charges should have a real impact on the level of public subsidy required. ORR said that over the period affected by the Regulator's review of access charges (until April 2001), this would result in savings to operators of some £1.5 billion compared with the current level of charges.

131. The DoT advised us of costs incurred during the rail privatisation process including specialist legal advice, merchant banking, accountancy and taxation, property, marketing, access charges, freight issues and information systems as well as running costs. The costs for the Department, OPRAF and ORR had reached £61.1m and would rise to £65m by 31 March 1995.[262] Costs incurred by Railtrack and BR owing to privatisation were estimated by the Department at £160m. BR said that £10m had been spent in 1992-93, £95m in 1993-94 (of which £49m related to the costs of setting up Railtrack), and that BR expected to spend about £78m on privatisation costs in 1994-95. These figures excluded new costs to the business arising from privatisation, such as licence fees (£3m).[263]

132. The Department estimated that by 31 March 1995 the total cost of privatisation would have risen from around £211m to approximately £240m. This figure included £30m expenditure on new computer equipment, some of which would have been needed in any case. The privatisation costs were, the Department told us, "a tiny proportion of the overall costs of the railway industry and are comparable to the costs of privatising other major nationalised industries". It was also argued that "As in the case of earlier privatisations, the modest costs involved will be more than outweighed over time by the resulting benefits to customers."[264] The breakdown of privatisation costs provided by the Department is shown in the following table.

---

[257]Q717

[258]Q60

[259]Q61

[260]Evidence, p.174.

[261]Evidence, p14, para 5.

[262]Evidence, p4, para 24.

[263]Evidence, p4, para 25; p11, Table 5; and p12, para 12.

[264]Evidence, p4, para 25.

TABLE 11[265]

Railway Privatisation Costs

	1991-92 £ million cash	1992-93 £ million cash	1993-94 £million cash	1994-95 £ million cash[1]	1995-96 £ million [1]	1996-97 £ million [1]	1997-98 £ million [1]
Department of Transport							
Running costs	0.5	1.2	1.5	2.2	2.8	1.3	0.9
Consultancy costs	0.5	5.5	10.5	12.0	11.8[3]	4.0[3]	1.0[3]
DoT total	1.0	6.7	13.5[4]	14.2	14.6	5.3	1.9
OPRAF							
Running costs	—	—	0.9	3.8	4.8[2]	3.8	3.8
Consultancy costs			1.5	12.8[2]	5.8	5.9	5.9
OPRAF total	—	—	2.4	16.6	10.6	9.7	9.7
ORR							
Running costs[5]	—	—	1.2	7.7[2]	8.2	6.5	6.5
Other costs			0.2	1.5	0.4	0.5	0.4
ORR total	—	—	1.4	9.2	8.6	7.0	6.9

Notes:

1. Estimated.
2. Indicative only; subject to funds being voted by Parliament.
3. Excludes the cost of consultancy advice on the flotation of Railtrack; these costs will depend on the extent of the sale and markets targetted, on which final decisions have yet to be taken.
4. Includes £1.5 million contribution by DoT to the costs of setting up OPRAF and ORR prior to formal appointments of Franchising Director and Rail Regulator.
5. Includes expenditure on consultants: outturn for 1993-94 was £0.6 million; forecast outturn for 1994-95 is £3.4 million. It is not possible to dis-aggregate planned expenditure on consultants from other running costs for 1995-96 onwards.

133. The Department's Annual Report puts these figures in the context of the whole industry:[266]

---

[265]Evidence, p.8, Annex E.

[266]Departmental running costs are excluded from these figures, taken from Figure 13, p21, *Transport Report 1995*, Cm 2806.

TABLE 12

Expenditure on the Railway Industry 1989-90 to 1997-98[1]

£ million	1989-90 outturn	1990-91 outturn	1991-92 outturn	1992-93 outturn	1993-94 outturn	1994-95 estimated outturn	1995-96 plans	1996-97 plans	1997-98 plans
Railway Industry									
National railways EFL[1]	646	917	1135	1606	1033	1279[2]	855	810	810
Union Railways & European Passenger Services EFL[2]	65	160	329	458	428	217	120	0	0
Total[4]	711	1077	1464	2064	1461	1496[2]	975	810	810
Other railway related									
Railway industry pensions[5]	71	58	61	72	54	45	22	22	22
Royal travel and railway grant audit	2	3	3	3	3	2	2	2	2
Payment of EU infrastructure grant to Union Railways	3			4	3	6	2	2	2
National Freight Company pension funds	6	7	7	9	9	8	8	8	8
National Freight Company travel concessions	2	2	2	2	3	3	3	3	3
Total[6]	84	70	72	90	72	64	37	37	37
Railway privatisation									
Total[6]				6	10	12	8	4	1
Total	795	1147	1536	2160	1543	1572	1020	851	848

1. Years 1989-90 to 1993-94 represent the External Finance Requirement (EFR); years 1994-95 to 1997-98 reflect the External Finance Limit (EFL).
2. The 1994-95 EFL may increase in-year by up to £64m.
3. 1995-96 EFL reflects a post budget transfer of £15m from EPS to Railtrack to fund investment undertaken by Railtrack on behalf of EPS. Figures also reflect the planned transfer of UR and EPS to the private sector during 1995-96.
4. EFLs from 1995-96 include £70m provision transferred to the Scottish Office to support services in Strathclyde PTE and do not show revenue effects of privatisation (see section 1.3).
5. Subject to adjustment.
6. Components may not sum to totals due to rounding.

---

[1]*DoT Annual Report 1995*, p.21.

VIII CONCLUSIONS

Railway Finances from 1994-95 to 1996-97

134. Our original decision to inquire into railway finances was prompted by concern about whether there would be a gap in the funding available to the railways in the financial year 1994-95 which has now finished. There was indeed a fall in BR's revenues as a result of the dispute between Railtrack and signalworkers last summer, loss of freight revenues and delays in the opening of the Channel Tunnel. These factors, as well as costs arising from privatisation, meant that the External Finance Limit set in November 1993 was insufficient. Late in 1994 the EFL for 1994-95 was set at £1,496m, £234m higher than forecast in 1993, and BR and Railtrack agreed to reduce their spending by £160m and £40m respectively (partly by reducing investment). This closed the gap substantially. In January 1995 there was a further relaxation bringing the final EFL for 1994-95 to £1,560m. These adjustments meant that railway services could be maintained at the level of the existing timetable during 1994-95.

135. The state of railway finances in 1995-96 and 1996-97 is much less clear because of the privatisation process. The Government intends to sell the BR Infrastructure Units (BRIS), freight companies, rolling stock companies (ROSCOs) and other BR businesses over this period, and the proceeds from these sales (though not that of Railtrack) are taken into account under the heading 'Privatisation Effects' in the Government's expenditure plans. This figure is the sum of privatisation proceeds from the sale of railway businesses minus the income lost by the privatisation of those assets. Thus although in 1995-96 the Government plans to pay £1,800m of grant through the Franchising Director and the Metropolitan Railway Grant, and the EFLs of European Passenger Services and Union Rail are together £120m, privatisation effects and external finance contributions from BR and Railtrack, as well as the transfer of £70m grant to the Scottish Office, produce a total railways EFL in 1995-96 of only £135m.[267]

136. Given the importance for the railway finances in the next few years of the privatisation of the businesses which until recently were part of BR, **we recommend that the Government publish in its reply to this Report a record of the dates for implementation of the various provisions of the Railways Act 1993 announced since the summer of 1992 by ministers and an explanation for any delay, and an up to date timetable for the sales of these railway businesses and a list of those already sold with, in the case of the latter, details of the proceeds of the sale and the corresponding loss of income to BR.**

137. The Government assures us that "the funds available to BR in 1995-96 will enable it to continue to provide services broadly in line with the current timetable and to meet its Passenger's Charter Standards."[268] We note, however, that among changes announced by BR to the May 1995 timetable are the abandonment of Motorail services and a substantial reduction in the number of sleeper trains. The RUCCs and Transport 2000 have also warned of cutbacks in services.[269]

138. As far as 1996-97 and 1997-98 are concerned, the Government told us that

"it is not possible at this stage to break down the BR/Railtrack EFLs for 1996-97 and 1997-98 into estimates of grant and individual EFCs; these figures will depend on a number of factors that will change as the process of privatisation proceeds. However, the Government is confident that sufficient funds will be available to ensure that its policy objectives of developing and improving the rail network and the services offered to rail users are achieved."[270]

---

[267]Evidence, p.3, para 17.

[268]Evidence, p.3, para 20.

[269]QQ407-408, Evidence, pp.195-6.

[270]Evidence, p.3, para 20.

Railway Finances in 1997-98

139. We have particularly focused on the question of whether there will be enough money to sustain services at about the level of the current timetable. The result of our consideration is reproduced as Figure 2 on page xix, and the assumptions and simplifications we have made are set out in paragraphs 40 to 43. As present assumptions are that privatisation will have been substantially completed by this time, profits of the businesses no longer return to the Government, and so the sums available to the Franchising Director and the PTEs to subsidise the railway system are essentially the same as the burden on the taxpayer. If costs and revenues get no better and no worse as a consequence of the franchising regime, this will need to be £1,760m at 1994-95 prices. We estimate that the sum of the grants available to the PTEs and the Franchising Director will be about £1 billion. In addition, the Franchising Director will have available a sum of £600m at 1997-98 prices shown as 'Privatisation Effects' in the DoT 1995 Transport Report, (about £560m at 1994-95 prices), which would go most of the way to closing the gap in funding. It seems that from 1997-98 onwards the Privatisation Effects sum will have to be treated as straightforward subsidy to operators if the financial structure of the privatised railway is to be sustained. **We recommend that in future expenditure plans the Government clarify matters by setting out the expected proceeds from privatisation sales and the total budget available to OPRAF as separate items.**

140. Even taking the Privatisation Effects figure into account, there appears to be a gap of £200m in the finances of the franchisees in 1997-98, based on Government estimates of grants in that year and on projections of current costs and revenues of the railways. At the moment it is not possible even for the Government to predict accurately the proceeds of all sales of railway businesses or the level of the franchise bids. However we must assume that the Government is optimistic that franchisees, by increasing revenue, growing their businesses and reducing costs, will be able to bridge that £200m gap. Certainly the Government regarded it as pessimistic to believe that there would be no improvement in operating costs or revenue performance over the next three years.[271]

141. As far as revenue is concerned, franchisees will obviously be keen to attract more passengers to use the railway. However overcrowding standards set by the Franchising Director on commuter lines, and capacity constraints on some regional services, may mean that in some cases, unless new rolling stock is purchased, there may be limited scope for revenue improvement from increasing passenger numbers. The recent announcement of caps on some fares, although welcome to passengers, will also limit the ability of franchisees to increase their revenues. Franchisees will in addition be the first to feel the financial effects of losses of patronage as a result of recession, industrial disputes, bad weather or other interruptions to services, and so will have to bear most of the revenue risk of the railways.

142. There is little doubt that efficiency gains and cost reductions can and will be made by franchisees. However, unlike some privatisations where costs have reduced very significantly, franchisees will not be in control of much of their cost base. Relatively long term contract payments to Railtrack and ROSCOs will typically amount to over 60% of their total costs. Traditionally railways have weathered recessions by reducing short term expenditure on infrastructure and rolling stock, but this option will no longer be available to franchisees. In addition, once a franchise has been let in a competitive bidding process it will not be open to a franchisee to reduce service quality. The Franchising Director has indicated that the service offered, as well as the price bid, will be taken into account in the award of the contract, so any attempt to reduce services once a franchise had been let would in effect amount to a breach of contract. **We believe that the Secretary of State and the Franchising Director should make this point clear to prospective franchisees before the franchising process continues.** There are therefore some factors that suggest that franchise bids will require additional public subsidy in order to reflect the constraints on train operating companies in managing the totality of their costs through the economic cycle. These factors could to some extent offset the benefits to the public purse of the efficiency gains and cost reductions which franchisees will make.

---

[271]Evidence, p.173.

143. We must assume that the 'Privatisation Effects' will be a permanent feature of the future financing of the railway, since they represent the annual cost of the permanent loss of revenue from railway businesses which have been sold, offset by the proceeds from their sale. These proceeds are to be obtained principally in the years 1995-96 and 1996-97. These businesses earn revenues in excess of £2 billion per year, and profits are initially guaranteed by leases of up to 10 years in the case of the ROSCOs. The effect of their sale will be a continuing £600m annual cost to public finances. We must therefore question whether these sales will represent good value for money to the taxpayer. However, since Government has told us that "the estimates underlying the figures for Privatisation Effects are commercially confidential", and that estimates of privatisation effects will be kept under review,[272] we can do no more than raise this question. It would be desirable for the Comptroller and Auditor General to review this matter. **We recommend that the Government provide detailed estimates of the total annual proceeds from the forthcoming privatisations of railway businesses, apart from Railtrack.** There can be no case for commercial confidentiality preventing these figures being made public, as they will be the sum totals of many businesses of different sizes.

Passenger Service Requirements

144. The Passenger Service Requirements (PSRs), which represent the services the Franchising Director is purchasing with his subsidy, are also important in any assessment of the future financing of the railway and of the future level of services for two reasons.

145. First, not all services which currently exist are to be included within the PSRs. This is partly because the Franchising Director wishes to allow some flexibility on high frequency routes, especially where these are provided on a commercial basis; he considered that "it would be inappropriate to take subsidy from the less well served parts of the network to safeguard these relatively frequent services should they become unviable".[273] It is also because "a relatively small number of specific services that are disproportionately expensive to run will not be included". Among these are the Motorail and sleeper services already mentioned.[274] Others are all the current InterCity services west of Swansea, which have not been included in the Great Western PSR on value for money grounds, although those routes will be covered by the PSRs for other franchises still be to announced.[275] Finally, some services which are currently included for purely operational reasons will not be specified in the PSRs.[276] We agree that franchisees must be allowed some flexibility in the provision of services and in operational matters. We also have no objection in principle to the omission of profitable services from PSRs, since it will be in franchisees' interests to provide them. **However, we would be concerned if a failure to specify loss-making services in Passenger Service Requirements led to those services disappearing. This could only be acceptable if either the money saved were used to support other services which were more heavily used or of higher value to passengers, or the amount of public subsidy paid to the railways were correspondingly reduced. What would be unacceptable would be for the same amount of subsidy to buy fewer rail services.** We return to this matter again below.

146. Second, the Franchising Director's evidence makes clear that if OPRAF's budget were cut to a level which was insufficient to meet the support commitments in the franchise agreements, then the Franchising Director would have to use a 'change procedure' to negotiate new Passenger Service Requirements reflecting the amount of money available.[277] **We draw attention to the fact that the Passenger Service Requirements are therefore not necessarily a guarantee of services in all circumstances.** The same difficulty would arise if OPRAF accepted bids for franchises that required more subsidy than BR is at present receiving. This could create pressure to cut back the PSRs set for later franchises to keep within the total budget. **We recommend that the Franchising Director's budget should be**

---

[272]Evidence, p.3, para 23.

[273]Evidence, p.17, paras 2.2 and 2.3.

[274]Evidence, p.17, paras 2.2 and 2.4.

[275]Q630.

[276]Evidence, p.17, para 2.5.

[277]Evidence, p.122-123.

allowed to increase if services are threatened simply because they are among the last to be franchised. We also recommend that the Franchising Director should always invite BR to bid for passenger franchises.

Government Support for Railway Services

147. The willingness of Government to commit itself to the future funding requirements of franchises over their whole life will therefore be crucial. Unless the Government feels able to bind itself to future spending the PSRs will not represent a guarantee of minimum levels of service. In addition, franchisees and other private participants in the railways will seek secure Government commitments of funding for the life of their franchises or contracts. **The Government should largely surrender the power to increase or decrease railway funding at short notice so that franchisees can obtain the backing of financial institutions to purchase companies or franchises or to fund the leasing of new rolling stock or infrastructure improvements.**

148. The total of grants paid to passenger train operators in 1994-95 via OPRAF and the PTEs was £2,157m, but BR was expected to pay back to the DoT £310m as profit and Railtrack will pay back £316m (Figure 1), giving a net cost of £1,531m to the public purse. In 1997-98, when we assume that the railway industry will have been privatised, profits will go to the shareholders, not the Department, although there will of course be payments to the Government in the form of corporation tax if the companies are profitable. We estimate the grant payable by the Franchising Director in 1997-98 to be £1,210m at 1994-95 prices, assuming that Privatisation Effects are, in fact, available to him as grants. The PTEs may contribute another £350m. The cost to the public purse after privatisation is therefore likely to be roughly the same as in 1994-95 at £1,560m if the Government's hopes for savings through franchising are realised, and rather more at £1,760m if they are not (Figure 2).

149. However, in 1993-94, before restructuring took place, the cost of grants to the taxpayer was only £1,073m (see para 23). Hence the privatisation process appears likely to result in an increase in public funding of about £500m to £700m a year. The Government will be relieved of the necessity to allow the railway to borrow from the National Loans Fund, but we have noted that the substantial borrowing by BR which was confined to the last four years was largely driven by the need to fund investment in Channel Tunnel services. **Assuming that the level and quality of services remains substantially unchanged, we question whether an increase in annual subsidy from roundly £1 billion in 1993-94 to over £1.5 billion in 1997-98 can be justified by the elimination of borrowing from the National Loans Fund for investment, given that BR required no such loans between 1981-82 and 1991-92.**

150. It is possible, of course, that in addition service levels may be lower in 1997-98, perhaps as a result of some franchisees operating only those services demanded by the PSRs. **In that case, we believe that the Comptroller and Auditor General should at that stage immediately examine the efficiency, economy and effectiveness of the policy of franchising services.**

Administrative Costs of Privatisation

151. BR and Railtrack had spent £160m on the administrative costs of privatisation by February 1995. The Department, OPRAF and the Office of the Rail Regulator had spent £65m by the end of 1994-95 and will spend a further £75m by 1997-98. The sums involved equal the purchase price of 80 four-car Networker trains. The DoT's view is that these costs are a small proportion of the cost of the railways and are comparable to the cost of privatising other major nationalised industries. It believed that the "modest costs" involved would be more than outweighed over time by the resulting benefits to customers. We have already seen that it is difficult at the moment to assess the levels of service that will exist, and their efficiency, when the railways have been privatised. It may well be that the private sector operators will be able to generate significant savings and efficiency gains. However, since the franchises and other contracts will first have to be let, these savings will accrue to the private railway businesses as profits unless the bids shortly to be received by OPRAF are significantly below the level of subsidy BR is currently receiving. The public purse may be unable to reap the benefits of some of these savings until the second round of franchising.

152. |Administration is only one of the additional costs generated by the implementation of the Railways Act 1993. These include the large increase in subsidy in 1994-95, in the form both of grant to the Franchising Director and Metropolitan Railway Grant, compared with the previous subsidy which, as already noted (paragraph 148), was by no means offset by the revised EFCs of BR and Railtrack. **We recommend that the Government publish as soon as possible details of the non-administration costs which have arisen as a result of the implementation of the Railways Act 1993.**

The Role of the Regulator

153. The Regulator has decided to cut the access charges to be levied by Railtrack by an initial 8% and a further 2% in each of the next five years. The effect of these cuts is to reduce the franchisees' need for subsidy by £1.5 billion over six years and therefore the cost to the public purse of supporting railway services. We consider that this decision, which the Regulator believes will allow Railtrack to spend £570m per annum on investment in renewals, is helpful; Railtrack should be able with this money to maintain the network in at least its current condition. We also welcome the Regulator's intention to harness Railtrack's property assets to the benefit both of Railtrack and operators.

154. The Regulator has at present no powers over the contracts between franchisees and the three rolling stock leasing companies (ROSCOs). This is despite the fact that there is almost no spare rolling stock on the network and that in practice, because much rolling stock is only suitable for use on certain lines, franchisees may have little real choice as to the source from which to lease their rolling stock. A monopoly situation therefore arises, at least until the market for rolling stock develops. While this may increase the sale price of the ROSCOs it may also increase the cost of letting the franchises. The Regulator told us that he would have no objection to being given regulatory authority over such contracts. We, too, believe that there would be merits in this in view of the absence of a real market in rolling stock. **We recommend that the Department give the Regulator powers in respect of contracts between franchisees and rolling stock leasing companies.**

Locally Supported Services

155. We have taken much evidence on the financial arrangements designed to ensure that the present level of PTE support for rail services can continue. We received evidence from PTEs and local authorities of the substantial increase in the cost of providing these services under the new railway structure. The Government realised this, and has introduced a temporary measure, Metropolitan Railway Grant (MRG), to top up funding to PTEs to allow services to bc provided at the same level as before restructuring. MRG will only be paid for the years 1994-95 and 1995-96, however. This is because it is set by reference to the cost of services before restructuring and to pay it indefinitely would be increasingly anachronistic.

156. The Government has made it clear that it does not want the PTEs to be out of pocket in supporting rail services simply because of a change in the railways' financial regime. It has therefore proposed to pay a new grant in the form of a 'bolt-on' to the relevant local authorities' standard spending assessment (SSA). This is believed by the Government to provide full compensation for higher costs but also to allow local authorities some discretion over whether in fact to allocate the funds to supporting rail services or to other areas of local authority spending. In addition the Secretary of State said that the Franchising Director could support services from which local authorities had withdrawn their support.

157. PTEs and local authorities were keen to have the arrangements for future funding confirmed quickly, or they might have to give notice to withdraw certain rail services in 1996. They had two concerns about the Government's proposals. First, there would be no certainty that all the extra money would be allocated to rail services, which required two or three times as much subsidy as before, and therefore offered poorer value for money. Second, the increased SSA would mean that some additional costs would fall on council taxpayers; only about 77% of the increased SSA would be available in the form of grant. The AMA calculated that local authorities might have to levy an extra £2 on the Band D council tax in order to make up this shortfall. We are however satisfied, as a result of seeing assurances

by the Department to the Association of Metropolitan Authorities,[278] that the arrangements for funding that will supersede Metropolitan Railway Grant will leave the local authorities with the resources to meet the increased costs of railway services without the need to raise additional funds from council taxpayers.

158. The Government's proposal will apparently allow local authorities to divert the extra money to supporting bus services or even to other areas of spending altogether, such as education. In most PTE areas there are some local authorities who receive far less benefit from supported rail services than others, and to them it may be very attractive not to spend this money on local railways. It is this uncertainty which has led to local authorities' reluctance to commit themselves to supporting some services in 1996 and could soon lead to notice being given of their cessation.

159. In recent years the PTEs have made an important contribution to developing their local rail networks and attracting passengers back to the railway. It is essential that they are fully compensated for the additional costs arising purely from the restructuring of the railways so that no additional burden is placed on the council taxpayer, and we welcome the Government's commitment to do so. The method it has chosen (Metropolitan Railway Grant) gives local authorities discretion whether to spend this extra money on railways or on other local authority services, which the Government believes is a positive advantage of the new system. In many cases, no doubt, authorities within PTE areas might be attracted to spending this money on supporting bus services or even on their non-transport services. The result of this greater discretion has, however, been an element of uncertainty as to future funding of rail services. Rail services inevitably involve long term commitments to rolling stock leasing and investment in infrastructure improvements and new stations. **It would be regrettable if uncertainty caused by the new system of funding PTE rail services caused the level of those services to decline.**

Freight

160. Freight volumes have fallen in recent years, in spite of the existence of grants to assist in the provision of rail infrastructure and, since last year, to subsidise up to 100% of Railtrack's access charges in the case of traffic which would otherwise go by road. Railtrack is obliged only to charge freight operators the avoidable costs of carrying traffic, but can charge more where it believes market conditions will allow this. Controls will be required to ensure that Railtrack actually does reduce its charges to the avoidable cost level in cases where Track Access Grant is claimed.

161. It remains to be seen whether the declining trend in freight volumes will be reversed following opening of the market to private companies, the privatisation of the three companies formed from BR's Trainload business and the opening of the Channel Tunnel. The Secretary of State thought there was potential for rail to carry more long distance, high value goods. We know of some obstacles, however: the Regulator's proposed insurance premiums, even for small freight companies, are high, locomotives and rolling stock are scarce and uncertainty over the future cost and availability of freight services may be affecting customer confidence. **We recommend that the Government consider whether there are any ways by which it could assist private freight companies faced with high insurance premiums and other barriers to entry which may be brought to its attention such as the availability of locomotives and rolling stock.**

---

[278]Letter from Mr John Watts MP to Councillor Dowd, AMA, 9 May 1995.

Investment

Infrastructure

162. Railtrack and the Regulator agree that the company needs to spend about £570m per year on renewals of the railway infrastructure in order to maintain the network in at least its present state. This is taken into account in the access charging regime which the Regulator has set. We welcome the fact that infrastructure renewal is to be ring-fenced in this way. Too often in the past investment has been cut in order to meet a shortfall in funds; under the new arrangements Railtrack should not find this necessary. **However, we believe that a proper assessment of the investment needs of Railtrack has been seriously hampered by the company's failure to publish its 10-year strategy which was promised to Parliament during the passage of the 1993 Railways Act. The Secretary of State should press the Chairman of Railtrack to publish this strategy as soon as possible.**

163. We received evidence from the railway equipment manufacturing industry, however, that orders from Railtrack for signalling and track components had fallen steeply since Railtrack was formed. For example, the RIA forecast that Railtrack would spend £37.6m with its members on signalling equipment in 1995-96. Railtrack, however, identified this as £44m and said it would spend a further £15m with other contractors. It believed that the RIA figures might be distorted by representing the turnover of the companies rather than the work done. Railtrack says it expects to spend £200m in total on signalling in 1995-96, half way between the RIA's estimate of the amount needed to maintain a 'steady state' and the amount needed to compensate for past underinvestment. It believed that its signalling renewals programme was consistent with the schedule of necessary works in the Hesketh Report as updated by its consultants. It was also keen to press ahead with the introduction of transmission-based signalling. **Despite the explanations offered by Railtrack, we find the size of the gap between the perceptions of Railtrack and the Railway Industry Association's members as to the volume of signalling work actually taking place a cause for concern.**

164. Similarly, the RIA gave evidence that purchases of rails, rail fastenings, switches and crossing had declined in the last two years to well below the average of European railways. Railtrack said that one of the main reasons for this was that the BRIS units were using up their inventories of such equipment; however, Railtrack did admit to a diminution in the amount of new track and pointwork being used. Railtrack would nevertheless spend about £200m per year on track renewals, the level BR regarded as the 'essential' level in order to maintain a 'steady state'. This would replace about 500 route miles.

165. There may be special, temporary reasons why Railtrack is purchasing less track equipment now than BR used to. However, we believe that if orders do not soon pick up from their present low level this will be a cause for concern. The Regulator has told us that he will monitor Railtrack's investment programme, and will consider reducing access charges in the event that Railtrack fails to deliver the capital investment it has agreed to undertake. Given the difficulty, as a result of the reorganisation of the railways, in comparing the past and present figures for investment spending, **we recommend that, when he satisfies himself that "Railtrack does not increase its profits by reducing expenditure on the renewal of assets below the level needed to deliver its obligations to operators",[279] the Regulator take into account the physical amount of work undertaken by Railtrack, and its orders for and use of track, electrification and signalling equipment, as well as the money spent. He should also take note of other indicators of Railtrack's output such as ride quality and the trend in the number of semi-permanent speed restrictions.**

166. **We also recommend that the Government should as soon as is practicable spell out the estimated proceeds from the privatisation of Railtrack and the proportion of these which will be made available for investment in railway infrastructure and rolling stock.**

---

[279]*Railtrack's Access Charges for Franchised Passenger Services: The Future Level of Charges*, Office of the Rail Regulator, January 1995, p.2.

167. The sale of the BRIS companies was welcomed by the RIA, although it expressed concern that they were now competing on favourable terms for work formerly undertaken by the private sector. This was, the Association thought, because the Government wished to sell the companies with full order books.

Rolling Stock

168. There were no calls for tender by BR in 1994-95 until 21 March 1995, when tenders to build about 40 Networkers were called for under the Private Finance Initiative. However neither tenderer submitted a compliant bid. This episode followed a decline in the level of rolling stock spending in the previous two years. This was partly the result of a conscious decision by BR in recent years, following a major programme of rolling stock replacement, to switch the emphasis of railway investment from rolling stock to the infrastructure.

169. The decline in rolling stock has had serious implications for ABB and, to a lesser extent, GEC Alsthom, the UK's two major passenger rail vehicle manufacturers. We were told in March 1995 that up to 1800 jobs were at risk within ABB without orders of about £350-400m per year, which was unlikely,[280] and 750 job losses were announced by the company on 11 May. The consensus of our witnesses was that while the responsibility for ordering trains would remain with BR for a little longer, it would pass to the ROSCOs when they were privatised. There would probably not be any large scale acquisition of new rolling stock by the ROSCOs until the franchised train operators were securely established.

170. There is thus the possibility of delays in the ordering of rolling stock while the new railway structure beds down. Even then, it is not clear how attractive such investment will be to franchisees; it will depend on the incentives which the Franchising Director is prepared to generate from his limited amount of subsidy. There also seem to us to be only weak incentives for the ROSCOs to purchase new rolling stock on a substantial scale; if the analogy of the bus industry after deregulation is anything to go by, they will initially be keen to manage their cash flow properly rather than renew their assets. The length of their (at present) unregulated contracts with the franchisees is also unlikely to be conducive to taking a long term view of investment, and may encourage the refurbishment of stock rather than its replacement. We believe that greater encouragement should be given to franchisees to lease new rolling stock. We are also concerned that manufacturers of rolling stock should not suffer a prolonged hiatus in orders purely as a result of the restructuring of the railways. **We therefore recommend that, while the new structure of the railway settles down, the Government require the Franchising Director to guarantee lease payments over more than one franchise period to encourage ROSCOs and other parties to acquire new rolling stock.**

Major Projects

171. Railtrack is keen to make progress on major investment projects such as Thameslink 2000 and, particularly, the upgrading of the West Coast Main Line on which it hopes to begin work during 1995-96. The modernisation of this line involves more than just infrastructure improvements, though: new rolling stock will also be needed if there is to be any improvement in journey times which are longer than on the East Coast and Great Western lines. The Franchising Director is the key player in ensuring that this upgrading occurs, as he is prepared to offer a long franchise (perhaps 20 years) to encourage the franchisee to pay for the investment in the infrastructure (through higher track access charges) and the rolling stock (by leasing from manufacturers who would also maintain the vehicles). **The modernisation of the West Coast Main Line, which the Secretary of State has reaffirmed remains a priority,[281] will be a test of the effectiveness and efficiency of the newly restructured railway, and particularly of the Franchising Director, in securing private finance to improve the condition of railway assets without undue delay.**

172. If a decision is made to modernise the West Coast Main Line using transmission-based signalling, which requires trains to be equipped with receiving and control equipment, many

---

[280]The 40 Networkers would have a capital value of about £150m.
[281]Q736.

other franchisees than just the West Coast Main Line Train Operating Company would be affected and would incur substantial costs. It is also far from clear that such a system would be available for use on a railway with a mixture of traffic within ten years (see para 96). The renewal of the West Coast Main Line is urgent, and reliance on an as yet unproven train control system to underpin the financial case for investment may lead to unacceptable delays in upgrading the nation's principal InterCity route.

Summary of Conclusions and Recommendations

173. Our principal conclusions and recommendations are as follows:

a) **We recommend that the Government publish in its reply to this Report a record of the dates for implementation of the various provisions of the Railways Act 1993 announced since the summer of 1992 by ministers and an explanation for any delay, and an up to date timetable for the sales of these railway businesses and a list of those already sold with, in the case of the latter, details of the proceeds of the sale and the corresponding loss of income to BR.** (Paragraph 136)

b) **We recommend that in future expenditure plans the Government set out the expected proceeds from privatisation sales and the total budget available to OPRAF as separate items.** (Paragraph 139)

c) **We believe that the Secretary of State and the Franchising Director should make clear to prospective franchisees, before the franchising process continues, that any attempt to reduce services once a franchise had been let would in effect amount to a breach of contract.** (Paragraph 142)

d) **We recommend that the Government provide detailed estimates of the total annual proceeds from the forthcoming privatisations of railway businesses, apart from Railtrack.** (Paragraph 143)

e) **We would be concerned if a failure to specify loss-making services in Passenger Service Requirements led to those services disappearing. This could only be acceptable if either the money saved were used to support other services which were more heavily used or of higher value to passengers, or the amount of public subsidy paid to the railways were correspondingly reduced. What would be unacceptable would be for the same amount of subsidy to buy fewer rail services.** (Paragraph 145)

f) **We draw attention to the fact that the Passenger Service Requirements are not necessarily a guarantee of services in all circumstances.** (Paragraph 146)

g) **We recommend that the Franchising Director's budget should be allowed to increase if services are threatened simply because they are among the last to be franchised. We also recommend that the Franchising Director should always invite BR to bid for passenger franchises.** (Paragraph 146)

h) **The Government should largely surrender the power to increase or decrease railway funding at short notice so that franchisees can obtain the backing of financial institutions to purchase companies or franchises or to fund the leasing of new rolling stock or infrastructure improvements.** (Paragraph 147)

i) **Assuming that the level and quality of services remains substantially unchanged, we question whether an increase in annual subsidy from roundly £1 billion in 1993-94 to over £1.5 billion in 1997-98 can be justified by the elimination of borrowing from the National Loans Fund for investment, given that BR required no such loans between 1981-82 and 1991-92.** (Paragraph 149)

j)   In the case that passenger service levels are lower in 1997-98 than now, but subsidies are higher in real terms, we believe that the Comptroller and Auditor General should at that stage immediately examine the efficiency, economy and effectiveness of the policy of franchising services. (Paragraph 150)

k)   We recommend that the Government publish as soon as possible deails of the non-administration costs which have arisen as a result of the implementation of the Railways Act 1993. (Paragraph 152)

l)   We recommend that the Department give the Regulator powers in respect of contracts between franchisees and rolling stock leasing companies. (Paragraph 154)

m)   It would be regrettable if uncertainty caused by the new system of funding PTE rail services caused the level of those services to decline. (Paragraph 159)

n)   We recommend that the Government consider whether there are any ways by which it could assist private freight companies faced with high insurance premiums and other barriers to entry which may be brought to its attention such as the availability of locomotives and rolling stock. (Paragraph 161)

o)   We believe that a proper assessment of the investment needs of Railtrack has been seriously hampered by the company's failure to publish its 10- year strategy which was promised to Parliament during the passage of the 1993 Railways Act. The Secretary of State should press the Chairman of Railtrack to publish this strategy as soon as possible. (Paragraph 162)

p)   Despite the explanations offered by Railtrack, we find the size of the gap between the perceptions of Railtrack and the Railway Industry Association's members as to the volume of signalling work actually taking place a cause for concern. (Paragraph 163)

q)   We recommend that, when he satisfies himself that "Railtrack does not increase its profits by reducing expenditure on the renewal of assets below the level needed to deliver its obligations to operators", the Regulator take into account the physical amount of work undertaken by Railtrack, and its orders for and use of track, electrification and signalling equipment, as well as the money spent. He should also take note of other indicators of Railtrack's output such as ride quality and the trend in the number of semi-permanent speed restrictions. (Paragraph 165)

r)   We recommend that the Government should as soon as is practicable spell out the estimated proceeds from the privatisation of Railtrack and the proportion of these which will be made available for investment in railway infrastructure and rolling stock. (Paragraph 166)

s)   We recommend that, while the new structure of the railway settles down, the Government require the Franchising Director to guarantee lease payments over more than one franchise period to encourage ROSCOs and other parties to acquire new rolling stock. (Paragraph 170)

t)   The modernisation of the West Coast Main Line, which the Secretary of State has reaffirmed remains a priority, will be a test of the effectiveness and efficiency of the newly restructured railway, and particularly of the Franchising Director, in securing private finance to improve the condition of railway assets without undue delay. (Paragraph 171)

GLOSSARY OF ABBREVIATIONS

AMA	Association of Metropolitan Authorities
BR	British Rail
BRIS	BR Infrastructure Services
DoT	Department of Transport
EFC	External Finance Contribution
EFL	External Finance Limit
EFR	External Finance Requirement
EPS	European Passenger Services
FTA	Freight Transport Association
ICWC	InterCity West Coast
MRG	Metropolitan Railway Grant
NLF	National Loans Fund
OPRAF	Office of Passenger Rail Franchising
ORR	Office of the Rail Regulator
PFI	Private Finance Initiative
PSO	Passenger Service Obligation (grant)
PSR	Passenger Service Requirement
PTA	Passenger Transport Authority
PTE	Passenger Transport Executive
RIA	Railway Industry Association
RFG	Rail Freight Group
RPI	Retail Price Index
ROSCO	Rolling Stock Company
RSG	Revenue Support Grant
SSA	Standard Spending Assessment
TOC	Train Operating Company (after vesting)
TOU	Train Operating Unit (before vesting)
WCML	West Coast Main Line

PROCEEDINGS OF THE COMMITTEE RELATING TO THE REPORT

Wednesday 5 July 1995

Members present:

Mr Paul Channon, in the Chair

Mr Matthew Banks	Mr Nick Hawkins
Mr Brian Donohoe	Mr Keith Hill
Mrs Gwyneth Dunwoody	Mr Andrew Mackinlay
Mr Paul Flynn	Sir David Madel
Sir Alan Haselhurst	

The Committee deliberated.

Draft Report (Railway Finances), proposed by the Chairman, brought up and read.

Ordered, That the draft Report be read a second time, paragraph by paragraph.

Paragraphs 1 to 145 read and agreed to.

Paragraph 146 read, as follows:

"146. Second, the Franchising Director's evidence makes clear that if OPRAF's budget were cut to a level which was insufficient to meet the support commitments in the franchise agreements, then the Franchising Director would have to use a 'change procedure' to negotiate new Passenger Service Requirements reflecting the amount of money available. **We draw attention to the fact that the Passenger Service Requirements are therefore not necessarily a guarantee of services in all circumstances.** The same difficulty would arise if OPRAF accepted bids for franchises that required more subsidy than BR is at present receiving. This could create pressure to cut back the PSRs set for later franchises to keep within the total budget. **We recommend that the Franchising Director's budget should be allowed to increase if services are threatened simply because they are among the last to be franchised.**"

Amendment proposed, in line 11, at the end to insert the words **"We also recommend that the Franchising Director should always invite BR to bid for passenger franchises"**.—(*Mr Keith Hill.*)

Question put, That the Amendment be made.

The Committee divided.

Ayes, 5	Noes, 4
Mr Brian Donohoe	Mr Matthew Banks
Mrs Gwyneth Dunwoody	Sir Alan Haselhurst
Mr Paul Flynn	Mr Nick Hawkins
Mr Keith Hill	Sir David Madel
Mr Andrew Mackinlay	

Paragraph, as amended, agreed to.

Paragraphs 147 to 173 read and agreed to.

Resolved, That the Report be the Fourth Report of the Committee to the House.

Ordered, That the Chairman do make the Report to the House.

Ordered, That the provisions of Standing Order No 116 (Select Committees (Reports)) be applied to the Report.

[Adjourned till Wednesday 12th July at a quarter to Four o'clock.

Printed in the United Kingdom for HMSO
Dd 5064453   C6   7/95   48003   H510570